Thomas Smith

The Life of a Fox, Written by Himself

And, Extracts From the Diary of a Huntsman

Thomas Smith

The Life of a Fox, Written by Himself
And, Extracts From the Diary of a Huntsman

ISBN/EAN: 9783337020309

Printed in Europe, USA, Canada, Australia, Japan

Cover: Foto ©ninafisch / pixelio.de

More available books at **www.hansebooks.com**

THE SPORTSMAN'S LIBRARY

EDITED BY

SIR HERBERT MAXWELL, Bart., M.P.

His heart and soul are in it.

Frontispiece.

THE LIFE OF A FOX

WRITTEN BY HIMSELF

AND

EXTRACTS

FROM THE

DIARY OF A HUNTSMAN

BY

THOMAS SMITH, ESQ.

LATE MASTER OF THE CRAVEN HOUNDS, AND AT PRESENT OF THE
PYTCHLEY, NORTHAMPTONSHIRE

*A NEW EDITION WITH THE AUTHOR'S ILLUSTRATIONS
AND COLOURED PLATES BY G. H. JALLAND*

EDWARD ARNOLD
Publisher to the India Office
LONDON NEW YORK
37 BEDFORD STREET 70 FIFTH AVENUE
1896

INTRODUCTION

More than eight centuries have rolled by since the attention of that keen sportsman, William our Conqueror, was drawn to the excellent hunting to be enjoyed in the land watered by the Avon, the Stour, and the Test, which caused him to mark off the New Forest as a royal chase, and ensure its preservation by laws of merciless severity. Never, since that distant time, has Hampshire lost its sporting pre-eminence among the southern counties; in spite of changing fashions and altered tastes, it still remains a perfect microcosm of English field sports. Fresh developments, indeed, have only served to bring out new points of excellence in this favoured county, for it is here that the latest refinement of modern sport—angling for trout with the dry fly—had its origin and may be enjoyed in the greatest perfection. The Normans, perhaps, had no time or mind for mere games; war, and the mimicry of war, were their only pastimes, except the sport of kings. But with the establishment of civil peace and in the leisure afforded by growing wealth and security, Hampshire men applied themselves to excel in games of strength and skill. Hambledon disputes with Mitcham, in Surrey, the honour of having been the cradle of the premier British game, cricket; and the world admires the ease with which, in these latter days, the men of Hampshire have applied themselves to golf.

Little wonder, then, that such a county, so rich in resources, and such a people, so ready to turn them to account, should have produced an abundant sporting literature. When the project of the *Sportsman's Library* was about to be carried into effect, it was to Hampshire that its Editor turned first, and the earliest volume of the series is the work of a Hampshire squire.

Stat magni nominis umbra—it would be difficult to hit upon a more thoroughly English name than Tom Smith. It was borne simultaneously by two celebrated sportsmen in Hampshire, namely, Thomas Assheton Smith of Tedworth and Thomas Smith of Hill Place. Each was a master of hounds for many years, and each had a whip called John Sharpe; so it is not surprising that confusion was common between the two Tom Smiths and the two John Sharpes.

The author of the following works was Thomas Smith, who lived at Hill Place, near Droxford, when he became master of the Hambledon Hounds in 1825. He hunted this country till 1829, when he took the Craven; afterwards becoming master of the Pytchley, at the time when the other Tom Smith was hunting the Quorn. In 1848 he took the Hambledon hounds a second time.

Now although, as has been shown, Hampshire has always been a hunting country in historic times, and probably long before them, it does not carry a high reputation among modern fox-hunters for the quality of its sport; it is far from being one of the flying countries. But in the Hambledon, Tom Smith hunted the best of the shire, and he certainly managed to show some wonderful sport in it. His performance in the Craven country, killing ninety foxes in ninety-one days hunting, is referred to with pardonable complacency in the preface to *The Diary of a Huntsman*; and, in fact, taking into account that it was achieved in what is notoriously one of the worst scenting countries in Great Britain, consisting in great part of woodland, this is a record which none but a first-class workman need attempt to emulate.

It is true that Tom Smith's method was not one on which everybody could look with favour. It used to be said that it was not the hounds that found a fox, but Tom Smith who found it for them, and, having found it, he hunted it for them also. "If I were a fox," said Mr. Codrington of the New Forest, "I'd sooner have a pack of hounds behind me than Tom Smith with a stick in his hand." But it is just this intimate knowledge of the habits of foxes and instinctive sympathy with their nature, that renders the *Life of a Fox* almost as interesting as if, as the title-page asserts, it really had been "written by himself."

As Nimrod, in his *Hunting Reminiscences*, has given what was probably a very faithful appreciation of Tom Smith in his capacity of M.F.H., it may be permitted to make the following extracts from that well-known work :—

Having seen a good deal of Mr. Smith in the field, and heard more, I hesitate not in calling him a very wonderful performer over a rough country; and although not what I call an elegant horseman—his seat being looser than I like to see it—no one can dispute his being a good one. Indeed everybody allows that, on a middling nag—and his have not been "from Alceste's royal stalls supplied"—he has few equals. He has not had, like his namesake, the means and opportunity of picking the best. However, I will go so far as to assert that, if I were asked for a subject to enable an artist to represent upon canvas the often-talked-of phenomenon of "a rum one to look at, but a devil to go," I should say, "Take Tom Smith's hog-maned black mare, with himself upon her," that is to say, if the said black mare be still in the land of the living. Believe me, reader, I mean no disparagement. On the contrary, as the bad carpenter never has good tools, so those of the more skilful one generally perform their office. I repeat, then, that Mr. Smith of the Craven is—all things considered—a surprising man across a country.

I have a more difficult task now to perform in drawing the character of this extraordinary huntsman, for extraordinary he certainly is, and in some respects unequalled by any man who has come under my observation in the character of a Master of Hounds, hunting them himself. And in what consists this striking peculiarity? I answer, first, in an enthusiastic zeal for, and an unsubdued spirit in, the pursuit of fox-hunting, which have carried him on in an almost uninterrupted prosperous course from the period when, as a schoolboy, he followed the hounds on his pony, to that which found him hunting the second best country in England. Secondly, there are features in Mr. Smith's character as a huntsman that appear to be peculiarly his own, and for which I have reason to believe the hunting world give him full credit. The sort of intuitive knowledge he displays in regard to what is called "the run of a hunted fox" may be said to border upon instinct. At all events, it is such as I have never seen or heard of in any other huntsman; and when we read in the preface to his book of his having killed ninety foxes in ninety-one days in the Craven country, we might almost say one half of them were killed by his hounds and the other half by himself. Then what is my opinion of Mr. Smith as a huntsman? It is told in a few words. He has proved that he can kill foxes with any man in England, and his having killed so many good old ones in his Hambledon country, and still more of all sorts in the Craven country, notoriously a bad scenting one, makes good the proverb that "handsome is that handsome does." Still I am compelled to say I am not a general admirer of Mr. Smith's system of hunting hounds—the system at least which he pursued when I saw him in the two countries above mentioned. There was too much wildness in his proceedings, too much of the *man*, if I may be allowed the expression, and not enough of the hounds, to satisfy a lover of hunting. I admit that there was something enthusiastically cheering in seeing him dash through a strong cover, come out of it with the leading hound and, with hat in hand and cheering halloo, ride away with the few couples that came next, apparently thinking nothing of those left behind. But where was his eye at this time?—on his hounds?—often not, but *forward* to some point which his intuitive knowledge of the line foxes take induced him to believe his had taken; and six times in ten he was right. But the question is, Is this the way a pack of hounds should get away from a cover with their fox? In my humble opinion it is not. It is not doing the thing altogether in a workmanlike[1] style, or in that in which fox-hunting should always be done. To carry on a scent *with safety*, the body of the pack should do the work, and this never can be the case when a few couples get away ahead, and the rest become blown in getting up to them. Neither is this system altogether favourable to sport. Foxes hallooed away and ridden after in this manner are very apt to run short, either from fear or from want of wind, a fact proved by the experience of woodland foxes generally standing *longer before* hounds than those found in gorse covers, because they most commonly have a chance to go *quietly* away. What is called bursting a fox, and

---

[1] "Workmanlike" it surely was, if the object of hunting be, as is commonly supposed it is, to kill foxes in the open. Nimrod should have used the epithet "artistic." But even from that point of view, there is something to be said in favour of Tom Smith's system, in a bad scenting country, by those at least who prefer a short gallop to puzzling out a cold scent over leagues of plough.—ED.

hunting him to death, are very different operations; and on this subject I can state an incident to the point which I witnessed with Lord Kintore's hounds in Scotland. We had run a fox about twenty minutes into a small cover, whence we viewed him breaking away again. "Pray help Joe to stop the hounds," said Lord Kintore to me, blowing his horn at the time, "*let him get well away and we shall have a run!*" He did get well away, with the body of the pack on his line; and the result was a beautiful forty minutes, and his brush is now in my view. I call this fox-hunting.

Let me not be supposed to have the least intention of detracting from the merits of Mr. Smith as a sportsman and a huntsman. The man who can kill ninety foxes in as many days, and in what Mr. Warde pronounced to be the worst scenting country he ever had to do with, must be allowed to be both one and the other. He had his system, and he found it answer; my only object in alluding to it is the desire that it may not become a precedent for those who come after him, and who may in vain attempt or expect, by similar means, the like success.

The Hambledon is certainly the best of all the Hampshire countries for hounds, unless it be the New Forest, and I saw a splendid run over it in Mr. Smith's time, of seventeen miles from point to point, without entering one cover, and the first fourteen without a cast; and in the same season he had one of the most remarkable runs that the annals of fox-hunting record, the description of it by Mr. Smith reminding one of the fox-hunting of olden times. The fact was, his foxes in those days took a lot of killing, and for this reason; previously to his taking the country, they had not been "killed down," as we term it, and the consequence was, a large portion of good old foxes able to stand before hounds.... I always admired Mr. Smith's conduct towards his field —firm without being offensive....

I cannot dismiss my notice of Mr. Smith, as a master of hounds, without offering a few remarks touching his book. I was disappointed in finding it so short. The announcement of the *Diary of a Huntsman*, —and of a huntsman of such long experience as Mr. Smith,—led me to believe I should get at least twice the information from it than is contained in the two hundred and twenty pages of large type and larger margin. I looked for the experience of some particular days, in which particular events had occurred, some particular difficulties been overcome; in fact, some new lights, and those by which masters and huntsmen, as well as others, might more clearly see their way in the dark and intricate path they take upon themselves to pursue in the difficult science of hunting the fox.

I think my friend—and in strict friendship I write this—is rather hypothetical on the cunning and *acquirements* of foxes, the latter the result of experience of good and bad scenting days, etc.; so, in my opinion, he also is on scent. Hypotheses are inseparable from so unfathomable a subject as that of scent; but to use the language of the fox-hunter, rather than the philosopher, the closer they hold on to the line, the better and more satisfactory they are.

Mr. Smith's chapter on hounds is the best in his book. It abounds in sensible, well-considered observations, which may be useful to the rising generation should fox-hunting last their time, of which at present there must be doubts in all reflecting minds. At all events, it is about to receive a "severe blow and great discouragement" in the combined effects of railroads, stag-hunting, and that abominably cruel and cocktail practice of steeple-chasing. I am glad to find Mr. Smith's opinion of the size of hounds for all countries agrees with that long since made known by me, which is in favour of those of large size, especially for severe countries. . . . Twenty-four inches for dog hounds against any other standard, say I. . . . The chapter by Mr. Smith on earth-stopping treats of a manner of performing this most essential operation, not generally known, and still less generally practised. If not carried on too far in the season, it has much to recommend it in theory; and as I am all for results in matters of this nature, the experience of its good effects by Mr. Smith, in the Craven country particularly, at once proves its usefulness in practice. Open earths are the great curse of fox-hunting, and in no country in which I have ever hunted has the evil been effectually done away with by merely trusting to occasional earth-stopping. Should Mr. Smith's plan of stopping at once for the season, or at least up to a certain period in it, not prove injurious to the breeding of foxes, it ought to become general.

I have printed Nimrod's criticism on the *Diary of a Huntsman* nearly *in extenso*, because it seemed more interesting to listen to the observations of a contemporary writer, especially to those of the famous Pomponius Ego, rather than to any retrospective remarks which might have occurred to myself. In fact, in some respects, Nimrod's reflections are nearly as instructive as the original work, read in the light of what has happened since his day. Fox-hunting has survived the fate which he suspected was to be brought upon it by railroads, stag-hunting, and steeple-chasing, all of which we have grown accustomed to look upon rather as allies of the Noble Science than as enemies; but we turn in vain to his pages for reassurance in respect to two dangers, of which he did not foresee the imminence, namely, the spread of wire-fencing, and political jealousy of an exclusive sport. Let us hope that fox-hunting may outlive these later perils, as it has survived the earlier ones.

In one matter the present generation of sportsmen may derive some consolation from Tom Smith's practical treatise. They are accustomed, no doubt, to hear modern principles and practice unfavourably compared with those of a bygone time. In fact, we have all been trained to regard, say, the thirties and forties as the golden age of fox-hunting. They were very good, no doubt, but Mr. Smith did not consider them equal to what had gone before. "It is true," he writes on page 199, "that old sportsmen beat men of the present day; *they* were trained, properly *entered* to hunting, and were taught to depend on their own eyes and ears," etc. But there is not too much of this *ætas parentum* sentiment in Smith's writing, just enough to reassure men of the present day when they hear their performances depreciated by fogies, who would be only too glad to exchange birthdays with them.

The disappointment expressed by Nimrod because the *Diary of a Huntsman*, first published in 1838, did not contain more episodes, was mitigated, perhaps, on the appearance five years later of the *Life of a Fox*. In that lively little work the author has made foxes from various countries recount what were, no doubt, his own experiences in pursuing them.

Tom Smith not only wrote so well that one is tempted to regret he did not write more, but he was a pretty draughtsman. There have not been many sporting authors whose illustrations stand reproduction so well, for instance, as the drawing of a good and a faulty hound (page 232), or the finish to a good run with the Hambledon hounds, depicted at page 252.

Tom Smith was something more than a fox-hunter; he was a close and accurate observer of nature, and his description of the *vie intime* of foxes was the outcome of a quick imagination served by a keen pair of eyes, rather than the hypothetical theorising to which Nimrod attributes it. Most of us must have heard the question discussed whether dew rises or falls. Smith solved the problem for himself (page 279), by simply taking note of the fact that, while the top of a gate may be covered with dew, the under side remains perfectly dry. Needless to say that meteorological science confirms the conclusion he arrived at independently, namely, that dew, being condensed vapour, falls out of the atmosphere and does not rise out of the earth.

In laying Mr. Smith's works once more before the public, the Editor has made none but a very few verbal alterations in them. In a few instances long footnotes have been incorporated in the text, and the profuse use of italics, to which writers and printers of sixty years ago were so prone, has been checked by the substitution of roman type, as being more agreeable to modern readers.

The story is current, how a certain noble lord, at present holding important office in Lord Salisbury's third administration, being anxious that his younger brother should prepare himself also to take part in public affairs, was urgent that the youth should not waste too much time over frivolous literature. Seeing him one day deeply engrossed in the perusal of a red-covered volume, Lord —— observed reproachfully that his brother would be much better employed in reading Lord Rosebery's *Life of Pitt*, which had just been published.

"All right, old fellow!" replied the younger man, "I'll read that too, but hadn't I better finish this first? It is the *Life of Fox*."

The book in question was Tom Smith's *Life of a Fox*.

In the present edition the author's drawings have been reproduced in facsimile, and coloured illustrations have been added by Mr. G. H. Jalland.   HERBERT MAXWELL.

MONREITH, 1896.

CONTENTS

THE LIFE OF A FOX

	PAGE
ADVERTISEMENT .	3
DEDICATION	5
THE LIFE OF A FOX	9
WILY'S STORY	11
COCK-TAIL'S STORY	58
CRAVEN'S STORY .	62
PYTCHLY'S STORY	68
DORSET'S STORY .	78
WARWICK'S STORY	87
CHESTER'S STORY .	94
DEVONIAN'S STORY	100
BERKSHIRE'S STORY	105
SANDY'S STORY .	110
CONCLUSION	133

THE LIFE OF A FOX

WRITTEN BY HIMSELF

B

WILY'S STORY. *Facing page 3.*

ADVERTISEMENT TO THE ORIGINAL EDITION

THIS little book may be looked upon as a curious manifestation of the movement among Foxes. The Editor ventures to send it forth, for an agreeable reminiscence to many who assisted in scenes which it describes; for some little instruction to sportsmen who have had less experience than himself; and for the common entertainment of all who like to listen to the way of the world in the woods.

HILL HOUSE, HAMBLEDON,
   10th June 1843.

To the Right Hon.
CHARLES, EARL OF HARDWICKE,
etc. etc. etc.

My Lord,—It is customary in a Dedication to use the language of fulsome adulation, even in cases where the writer and the person addressed affect an equal abhorrence of it. Adopting a more simple, straightforward course, and one more worthy of my name, for few foxes have run more straight, I will candidly inform your Lordship that the love I bear you is much the same as that borne to myself by the most venerable hen now cackling in your farmyard, whose half-fledged brood I have often thinned. But, my Lord, although I openly acknowledge my aversion to the unfeathered biped species to which you belong, yet the kinds and degrees of hatred are various as the characters of those towards whom we entertain it; and while some, affecting to treat my persecuted race as noxious vermin, destroy us by day and by night with snare, trap, gun, and every other engine which their ingenuity can devise, we have always found in your Lordship a fair and open enemy, and one who disdained to have recourse to the cowardly contrivances above referred to. It is on this account, my Lord, that I have done you the honour to dedicate to you the following narrative of my eventful life.

Many are the happy hours that I have spent, some years since, in the neighbourhood of your Lordship's hen-roost in Hampshire, and latterly many a tender rabbit, etc., have I carried home from the plantations and fields which you now so handsomely preserve for the use of myself and my kindred at Wimpole; this conduct on your part would have ensured my lasting gratitude, could I forget how frequently I have been driven by hound and horn from those treacherous coverts. Although, from the above reasons, there cannot be friendship between us, there may, I trust there does, exist some feeling of mutual respect; you and your brethren are not insensible to those merits in our species which you affect to depreciate. Fabulists and other writers, in all languages, have quoted the sayings and doings of my ancestors, as lessons of instruction for youth; while the craft and cunning of your ablest statesmen have been, in many instances, entirely derived from our acknowledged principles and practice. Our heroism in the endurance of a violent and cruel death is equalled only by our dexterity in avoiding it. It was only last winter that a cousin of mine led a gallant field of two hundred horsemen over thirty miles of the finest country in England; and when at length overtaken by twenty couple of his enemies, each one larger and stronger than himself, he died amid their murderous fangs, without suffering a yell or cry to escape him! Yet do the poets of your race celebrate as a hero, one Hector, *a timid biped*, who, after a miserable run round the walls of

Troy, suffered himself to be overtaken and killed by a single opponent!

Such, my Lord, is the justice of historic fame in this world, wherein thousands of men have written; whilst I alone of my tribe have been endowed with the power of thus using the quills of that excellent bird, which has been for centuries the favourite object of pursuit amongst the brave and skilful of my race.

However determined I still may be to trespass upon your Lordship's preserves, I will do so no longer upon your time. Our walks in life are different; 'tis yours to ride, 'tis mine to run; 'tis yours to pursue, 'tis mine to be pursued; we shall meet again in the field, the horn will sound the alarm, my appearance will be greeted with a view-halloo that shall set the blood of hundreds in motion! Whether after that day of trial I shall again sit amongst my listening cubs, and relate to them how many peers, parsons, and squires lay prostrate on the turf, and were soused in the brook while pursuing my glorious course, or whether my brush shall at length adorn your Lordship's hat, fate must decide.—Meanwhile I remain, your Lordship's obliged friend,

WILY.

MAIN EARTH, *6th June* 1843.

THE LIFE OF A FOX

A FAITHFUL history of the life even of a Fox may be not without its interest, for, to the wise, nothing in nature is mean, and truth is never insignificant. I was prompted to write this account of myself by overhearing one day, as I lay in a covert by the roadside, the following remarks by one of a party who were passing by on their return home from hunting a fox, which, as it appeared, the hounds had failed to kill.

"Well, I'd give a good deal to know what became of our fox,—how was it he could have beaten us? There is nothing I should like better than to invite to supper all the foxes that have escaped from packs by which they have been respectively hunted to-day, and then persuade them to declare to what cause they owed their escape. To tempt them there should be rabbits at top, rabbits at bottom and sides, rabbits curried, fricasseed, and rabbits dressed in every imaginable way, by the best French cook."

The thought pleased me, and resolving to gratify my own curiosity, I invited all of my friends who had at any time beaten some pack of repute.

It was a fine moonlight night, in the middle of summer, when ten of my guests, besides an interloper, a stranger to us all, arrived at the place appointed, beneath an old oak tree in the New Forest.

For the foundation of my feast, nothing could be better than the bill of fare projected by the hospitable hunter; but as I knew that my friends would prefer everything *au naturel*, I dispensed with the services of M. Soyer, and merely added, for the sake of variety, some fine rats and mice, a profusion of beetles, and a bird or two for the few whose taste might be depraved enough to choose them. Our repast being over, it was agreed, that for our mutual instruction and entertainment, each in his turn should with scrupulous fidelity relate by what arts and stratagems, or by what effort of strength and courage, he had eluded and baffled those ruthless disturbers of our repose, the huntsman and his hounds. I was first called on to tell the story of my life, and thus began.

T. Smith, Esq. del. *Fairy page 1*

WOLF ADDRESSING HIS FRIENDS.

WILY'S STORY

I AM descended from the ancient family of the Wilys, and was born on the 25th day of March, in the year ——. Within three or four weeks from that day of the year every fox of us in this country is probably brought forth; and it seems especially designed that the female should thus produce her only litter in the year at a season when our favourite food, young rabbits, are most abundant. The spot in which I first drew breath was a breeding-earth, carefully chosen by my mother, in a well-known covert, called Park Coppice, situated in the centre of the Hampshire Hunt. It was not until the tenth day after my birth that I first saw light, or acquired sufficient strength to crawl with safety to any little distance round our nest. Had I earlier possessed the use of sight, I might have strayed beyond my warm shelter, and for want of sufficient strength to return to it, have perished with cold. Thus Nature goes on to care for us. I had two brothers and two sisters, and we all throve and grew rapidly with the nourishment of our mother's milk alone, until we were six weeks old, when she began to supply us with other food, such as rabbits, and rats and mice, which she tore to pieces and divided amongst us in equal shares, not however so much to our satisfaction as to prevent our snarling and quarrelling with each other thus early over our meals. That part of the earth where we lodged was between two and three feet square, with several passages just large enough for our mother to crawl along; several of these crossed each other, and of two that terminated outwards one only was used by our mother, who stopped up the other for times of emergency. In these several passages we daily amused ourselves with chasing each other round and round. On one occasion we were interrupted in the midst of our gambols by the sudden entrance of our mother, who seized us with her sharp teeth, and carried us to the back of the earth. It seemed that she had been watching outside, for immediately after this we were alarmed by a sound hitherto unheard by us. It was the voice of a man crying out, "Eloo in, Viper! fetch 'em out! hie in there, hie in!" The light was instantly shut out by the intrusion of a dog in a low and narrow part of the passage, which compelled him to crawl along with his head to the bottom. Our mother waited for him, where she had the advantage of higher space, and as he approached with his head thus low, she fixed her teeth across the upper part of his nose and pinned him to the bottom of the passage, where she held him so that he could not bite her, which he would have done had she attacked him after he had got beyond the lower part, when he might have raised his head up.[1] Whilst bleeding and howling with agony, he drew her backwards to the opening, where she let him go. It was in vain that the man tried to make him go in again, and so he left the

---

[1] If this were attended to in making artificial earths, it would be an advantage to the fox, who might then defend himself better from dogs of every sort; the great point is to have the entrance *only just sufficiently high* for him to get in.

They should be so arranged that the breeding places are situated higher than the entrances, so that water may run away; and when it is necessary to make the earth on level ground, the breeding places should be on the surface, and covered over with earth, so as to form a mound.

The places for breeding should be formed in a circle, in order that

place, declaring his conviction that there were cubs within, and that he would have them out another day. He was, however, disappointed, for our mother that night took us one by one to a large earth in a neighbouring wood. We were now two months old, and ceased to draw our mother's milk, which we no longer needed, as we were able to kill a rabbit or pluck the feathers of a fowl when she brought it to us, as well as she. Some of these feathers, which in our frolics we had carried to the mouth of the earth, once betrayed us to a couple of poachers, who had been lurking about the wood, and who noticing them, procured a long stick and thrust it into the earth, nearly breaking the ribs of one of my brothers. When they pulled it out again, they found the end of it covered with his hairs. This satisfied them, and leaving us scrambling and huddling together up to the back of the earth, they went away, resolving to come back next day with tools to unearth us, and expecting, as they said, to sell us for half-a-guinea apiece.

they may be more easily arched, like an oven, without having wood supports.

The passages should be floored with bricks or flints, to prevent rabbits from digging.

It is desirable to have the low passages not more than seven inches high, to exclude dogs. Four-inch work at the sides is sufficient, except for a foot or two at the entrance.

" 'Twas a 'nation pity," added one of them, "we hadn't brought my little terrier, Vick; she would have fetched 'em out alive in her mouth, without our having the trouble of digging, though they was as big as the old 'un."

"Mind," said the other, "we beant seen, or else the squire will gie us notice to keep off."

Their intentions were defeated; for our mother, who had been all the time watching their goings on, anxiously waited for their departure, and no sooner had night set in than she again removed us to a gorse-covert hard by, and placed us in a nicely-sheltered spot, where she herself had often lain before. Here we were safe from poaching kidnappers, as it would have been impossible for them to find us without being found out themselves whilst searching for us. Let every mother lay up her cubs in gorse, or close and thick coverts, rather than in large earths, which are sure to be well known to the fox-taker. We were now three months old, and living upon young rabbits and mice, with which such coverts abound, feeding also upon other food, such as black beetles; rabbits, however, were our favourite food, and if we could find them, we cared for little else. They are fruitful breeders, particularly at this season of the year; and a female has been known to carry two distinct broods of young at the same time, and to bring them forth three weeks after one another. This astonishing fact I have witnessed myself, and I have heard that the same thing has occurred with the female hare. The usual time of bearing is twenty-eight days. We now began to venture out of the covert at nightfall, or even before, being warned by our mother, whenever there was danger, with a peculiar noise that she made, like "keck, keck"; which we no sooner heard than we were out of sight in the covert, where we stayed until all was still again.

As we grew older we grew more bold and more cunning; and being four months old, ventured farther abroad, even in the day-time, entering the fields of standing corn, until it was cut down, when the deeds we did there were suddenly brought to light.

"Why, John," says the farmer, "there must be some young foxes hereabouts; look at the rabbits' feet lying about; and what's the meaning of all these white feathers? This comes of not locking up the fowls o' nights. Never blame the foxes, poor craturs; but just go to the kennel, and tell

Foster, the huntsman, as soon as the corn is off, to bring his hounds."

"Very well, sir."

"But mind, he ain't to kill more than one of 'em, or else be hanged if ever I takes care of another litter."

All this was explained to me afterwards, for at the time I did not understand much about it. I only knew that the speaker was a very nice sort of man, and never doubted that he meant everything that is pleasant; although I must say that his outward looks, the first time I saw him, did not at all take my fancy. There appeared to me something so ungainly and unnatural—something so very absurd, to see an animal reared up on end, and walking about on his hind legs; to say nothing of what seemed his hide which hung about him in such a loose and uncouth fashion, as if nature had been sick of her job, and refused to finish it.

A few evenings after this I was crossing a field, and watching some young rabbits, with which I longed to become more nearly acquainted, when suddenly a large black dog and an ugly beast called a gamekeeper, jumped over a hedge. I immediately lay flat on the ground, hoping that I should not be seen; when, however, I found them coming within a few yards of me, I started off, closely pursued by the villainous dog, and seeing that I should soon be overtaken, turned round, and slipt away between his legs. I then made towards the hedge, and the dog springing after me, I suddenly turned round again, when he, trying to do the same, tumbled heels over head, and nearly broke his precious neck. My comfort was to think that he was certainly born to be hanged, for he followed me again as if nothing was the matter, and soon overtaking me, wearied as I was with the sport (I think they call it), he seized me by the back of the neck, and jogged away with me in his mouth to his master, who clapped me into his enormous pocket, and carried me home. I was kept there in a dark and dirty place, where all sorts of animals had been kept before. There I remained, who by nature am the cleanliest of animals, with my hairs all clotted with mire and filthy moisture, and should certainly have perished of a certain loathsome sickness, had not another gamekeeper luckily seen me, and told my owner the certain consequence of keeping me so. I was then taken out and put into a hamper out of doors, ready to be carried by the night-coach to London for sale. After trying in vain to gnaw a hole for my escape, I set about making all the noise I could, which, the night being still, reached the ears of my mother, who quickly came and helped me with her teeth to finish the work which I had begun, and so I got out and away.

Having thus suffered for my boldness, I scarcely ever ventured out of the covert till dark, or nearly so; generally, indeed, I remained in my kennel the whole of the day, unless I had not been fortunate in procuring food the night before. I have seen a female fox, when she had young ones, moving about earlier in the afternoon; otherwise it is contrary to our habits to do so. Night is more dear to us than day, and the tempest suits our plans; for man is then disposed to keep quiet, and we venture more boldly to approach his dwellings in search of stray poultry, which are to be found abroad, not having been driven into the hen-roost, owing to the neglect of their owners.

I resolved to accompany my mother in future as much as possible in her excursions, that I might profit by her prudence and observe her ways. She seldom went abroad till night, though sometimes she would venture in the dusk of evening. Upon one occasion I was much amused with an example of her engaging tricks. It was a bright moonlight night when I saw her go into a field, in which many rabbits and hares were feeding. On first seeing her, some of them ran away for a few yards, some sat up on their hind legs and gazed at her, and some squatted close to the ground. My mother at first trotted on gently, as if not observing them; she then lay down and rolled on her back, then got up and shook herself; and so she went on till the simple creatures, cheated by a show of simplicity, and never dreaming she could be bent on anything beyond such harmless diversion, fell to feeding again, when she quietly leaped amongst them and carried off an easy prey.

We were now fully able to gain our own subsistance, but not the less would she watch over our safety. One of my brothers having found a piece of raw meat had begun to devour it, which she observing ran forwards, and as if in anger drove him away from it. He became sick and lost all his hairs, owing to poison, which I afterwards learnt had been put in the meat. It was fortunate for us that we had left the breeding-earth, for we must otherwise have all been infected with the same noisome disease, the mange. By first smelling it, and then turning away, she taught us in future to avoid anything of the kind that had been touched by the human hand. Thus when we happened to be smelling with our noses to a bait covered over

with leaves, moss, grass, or fine earth, she would
caution us to let it alone by her manner of looking
about, as if she were alarmed and expected to see
our enemy the keeper. Sometimes the iron trap
would be seen; and then she would lead us to look
at and smell it. Our noses, however, would not
always be a safeguard, for after the trap has been
laid some days, particularly if washed by rain, the
taint of the evil hand would be gone, and though
we ourselves, thanks to the watchfulness of our
mother, escaped the danger, hundreds of others, led
on by hunger, have fallen into the snare, losing
either leg or toes. Baits for catching stoats and
weasels, set upon a stick some fourteen inches above
the ground, we carried away without mischief from
the trap below. At about six months old we were
three parts grown, I and my brothers being something larger than our sisters, whose heads were
thinner and more pointed. The white tip of the
brush was not, let me remark, peculiar to either
sex of us. I and one of my brothers, and also one
of my sisters, had it whilst the other sister and the
other brother were altogether without it, not having
a single white hair. That brother has been known
to profit by the exemption, when on being viewed
in the spring of the year the hounds have been

stopped with the remark, "It's a vixen; there is no white on her brush." I have since observed that old male foxes are of a much lighter colour on the back than are the old female ones, which are commonly of a dark reddish brown; and so it was with my parents. Our sire never helped to furnish us with food, although I have reason to think that I often saw him prowling about with my mother at night; instances, however, have been known where the sire has discharged such an office after the young had lost their mother. For a few weeks we went on living a rollicking kind of life, and fancied ourselves masters of the coverts.

There was a coppice of no more than two years' growth, which enabled me to enjoy the beams of the sun as I lay in my kennel. This kind of shelter we all of us choose, especially when there are no trees of a large growth to be dripping down upon us in wet weather. Here as I lay one morning, early in October, I was roused from a sound sleep by the noise of voices, and of dogs rushing towards me. Away I ran, and had not gone above twenty yards before I heard the report of a gun, and instantly received a smart blow on my side, which nearly knocked me down, breaking however none of my bones, and causing only a little pain and loss of blood.

"Ponto!—curse that dog; he's after him," cried a voice, when the dog turned back, or else he must certainly have caught me, as I had only power to run a short distance into some thick bushes, where I lay down and listened to the following rebuke.

"You young rascal, how dared you to shoot at a fox—here, too, above all places? Don't you know that this is the very centre of the hunt? Had you killed him, you would have been a lost man, an outcast from the society of all good people, a branded vulpicide. Who do you think that has the slightest regard for his own character would have received you after that?"

"I really," replied the offending youth, "mistook him for a hare."

"Yes, and if you had killed such a hare, you should have eaten him, and without currant jelly too."

Now, if an humble individual of a fox may venture to give an opinion upon such a momentous question, I will say that the practice of destroying our breed for the purpose of preserving the quantity of game, is, where it prevails, equally selfish and short-sighted. For every fox thus destroyed hundreds of men are deprived of a day's sport, and sometimes more than that; and if none of us were spared, those hundreds of hunters would become so many keen shooters—how could the game-preserver then keep up his stock as he did before? And where would the wealthy capitalist rent his manor? After this unlucky adventure I resolved in future to sleep with one eye open, and not without reason. I had scarcely recovered from the injuries which I had suffered, and had just settled in my kennel one morning about daybreak, coiling myself up for the usual snooze all day, and sticking my nose into the upper part of the root of my brush—the reason by the bye why the hairs there are generally seen to be standing on end or turned backwards—when I was startled by the voice of John Foster, whose name has been mentioned before: "Eloo in; e-dhoick, e-dhoick, in-hoick, in-hoick." Disturbed by the unaccustomed sounds, I rose upon my fore-legs, and pricking up my ears listened for a moment or two, when I heard the rustling of the hounds running straight towards me, being led on by the scent that was left in the track of my feet, which parts, especially when heated by running, seem to leave more scent than any other part of the body. Thus the same organ becomes at once the means of inviting pursuit, and of escaping it. Off I went—the awful tongue of an old hound ringing in my ear, and having about it surely some charm; for no sooner had he opened than a score or two others of the pack came rushing from all sides towards him, and then such a horrible din as there was behind me. I ran—I flew, I knew not whither—I crossed a road in the wood—and then such frantic screaming and shouting—"Tally-ho! tally-ho!" mixed with the blast of Foster's horn, that I was almost mad with fright, and must have fallen a victim to my savage pursuers, had not my brothers and sisters been disturbed by the clamour, and consequently been the cause of the pack being divided into several parts, thus enabling me to steal away towards the opposite side of the wood, where I remained. My state was such that I could not be still, as I ought, and I kept moving backwards and forwards and away from the cry of the hounds, which at times hunted us in several packs, then all together as they crossed each other, and then again separated. This had gone on for nearly half an hour when, to my great joy, they all went away with a frightful yell, leaving the wood and me miles behind them. I was congratulating myself on my escape, and listening to hear if they were returning, when I was startled by the sound of steps approaching, and a panting, as of some animal in distress; it was one of my brothers, evidently more beaten and terrified than myself, and who, on hearing something move and not knowing it was I, ran back out of sight in a moment, and I saw no more of him then. I remained where I was hidden until I had partly recovered from my fears, and not hearing the noise of hounds, had crept into some thick bushes, where I lay quiet, when to my horror I again heard the halloo of the huntsman, who seemed to be taking the hounds round the wood, with now and then the tongue of a single hound; then, all on a sudden the deep voice of Sawyer, the whipper-in, calling, "Tally-ho! there he goes; 'tis a mangy cub!" In a minute every hound was after him, and in full cry for a quarter of an hour; suddenly the noise ceased, and the fatal halloo, "Whoop!" was often repeated by the men with "Tear him, boys; whoop! whoop!" And that was the end of my poor, mangy brother. They then, not having seen any other of us for some time, thought we were gone to ground, and went away. Happy was I to hear that horn, which had before caused me such terror, calling away the hounds, that, to judge from their loud breathing as they passed near me, were not loath to go, for it was nearly ten o'clock, and the heat most oppressive. They were mistaken in thinking we were all gone away, although my brother and sisters had taken advantage of the hounds running in the open, and had gone across to the gorse-covert, from which my unfortunate brother just killed had often, in consequence of his mangy state, been driven by our mother. Again we had to thank that mother for our safety, for at the time when we were all nearly dead with toil and alarm, it seems she took an opportunity of running across the wood in front of the hounds, which soon got on her scent, and followed her as she led them away for some miles out of the covert. The huntsman then, convinced that they had got on an old fox, as soon as the men could stop the hounds, immediately brought them back to the covert where they had left us, hoping to kill one of us young ones.

It was not till some time after this memorable day that we ventured to take up our quarters in the wood again. Our mother thought it right to take us away to a covert about two miles distant, where, as the hounds only hunted cubs at this early part of the season, there were no young foxes; consequently, for that time, we were left undisturbed, and soon began to feel as much at home as in the covert which we had left. Had it not been for the shooters who frequently came with their spaniels, we should have even preferred it; and they so frequently moved us that we soon took little notice of them, except by going from one part of the wood to the other. Indeed, we were rather benefited by them than otherwise, for we occasionally picked up a wounded or dead bird, hare, or rabbit, and after eating as much as we could, we always buried the remainder, scratching a hole in the ground with our claws, and covering it over with earth. Even this made us enemies; for when by accident the dogs smelt it, and drew it out, the keepers immediately told their master that if they were not allowed to kill the foxes, there would not be a head of game left.

Constant disturbance after this induced us to return to the strong gorse where we had previously been, and which was nearly impenetrable by shooters; but we had not been here more than a few days, when, about ten o'clock in the morning, towards the end of October, I was again alarmed by hearing Foster the huntsman's now well-known voice: "Sawyer, get round the other side of the covert; if an old fox breaks away, let him go, stop the hounds, and clap them back into the covert again, and then they will get settled to a cub. In-hoick! e-dhoick! e-dhoick!" I listened with breathless fear, and soon heard the rustling of hounds on every side of me, then a solitary slight whimpering, and Foster's cheer, "Have at him, Truemaid; hoick! hoick!" These sounds, frightful in my ears, sent every hound to the same spot; and I started from my kennel, and got as fast as I could to the other side of the gorse. I soon gladly returned, and meeting an old dog-fox that at first I mistook for a hound, dashed away on one side before the pack had crossed my line. They ran by me, and continued following the old fox, till I heard "Tally-ho! gone away"; with a smacking of whips, and "Hoick back, hoick back"; then for a few minutes all silent; and then again the same terrible tongues drove me from my quarters. They were not in pursuit of me in particular, but running after either my mother or one of the rest or all of us, divided as they were into different lots. One of these at last got fast on my track, and away I went straight to the earth where we were born; but to my surprise and disappointment I found it stopped up with a bundle of sticks, and covered over with fresh earth; for it was not in that state when I passed by it the night before. I waited for a few moments, and tried to scratch an opening; but hearing the hounds hunting towards me, I returned to the gorse, where they shortly followed me. Owing to my being smaller than they were, I could easily run a good pace in it, where they were obliged to go slowly; and running in the most unfrequented tracks, I contrived to keep out of their way. At times they were all quite silent, and could not hunt my scent at all, owing probably to the ground and covert where the hounds had been running so often being stained. This dreadful state of things went on for a length of time, till at last I heard them halloo "Tally-ho! tally-ho! gone away." Shortly after this the hounds left the covert, hunting after the fox which was seen to go away, and which again happened to be our mother. The men soon found out their mistake; and as they were some time absent, they must have had difficulty in stopping them, which at first I heard them trying to do.

Meanwhile I had been flattering myself that I was safe, and that once more I had escaped; but quickly I heard them coming back very quietly, as if intending again to hunt me. Previously to this I had found a rabbits' burrow, into which I crept. I was luckily, as it happened, too much distressed and too heated to remain there, and left it, and went to the opposite side of the covert. At this time a cold storm of wind and rain came on, notwithstanding which an old hound or two got on my line of scent, and hunted it back the contrary way to that which I had gone, till they came to the rabbit burrow, where they stopped, and began baying and scratching with their feet at the entrance.

There can be little doubt that hounds have a language well understood by each other, and I never can forget the noise made by the whole pack as they all immediately came to the spot; the men hallooed " Whoop! whoop! have at him, my lads"; and one was ordered to fetch a terrier, and tools for digging. During the time they were at this, I stole away from the covert in another direction, and so saved my life. It seems they soon found out that I had left the earth, tried the covert over again, and then went home, vowing my destruction another day.

This was warning enough to prevent my remaining longer in or near this covert for the present. Venturing farther abroad, I returned to that in which I had been disturbed by the shooters, and there frequently picked up more wounded birds; I also found, in a field close by, part of a dead sheep, which a shepherd had left for his dog. Some of this I took away and buried. I was returning for another bit, when the rough dog, which had just arrived, suspecting that I had purloined his meat, flew at me the instant he saw me with such fury that he knocked me over and over again without getting hold of me. He then turned, and was in the act of securing me with his teeth, when I griped one of his legs and bit it through; the pain which he suffered prevented him from more than mumbling me with his teeth; so I got off, and made the best of my way to the covert that evening.

I felt next day that, bruised as I was, I could not have escaped for ten minutes from a pack of hounds had they found me; I therefore lost no time in reaching a main earth, into which I got before the earth-stopper had put to; but I had scarcely done so when he came at daylight, and to my great dismay stopped it up. I remained there all day and till late at night, and no one came to open it, and had I not contrived to scratch my way out, I know not how long I might have remained there, for I have reason to know that many of us are stopped up in rocky earths and drains for weeks, and starved to death, owing to the forgetfulness or sheer cruelty of the stoppers. I have heard such sad tales as—but just now it would interrupt my story to tell them.

It so happened, my friends, that for some time

I was not hunted by hounds, and contrived to extend my rambles till I was acquainted with a great part of the country. Occasionally lying in my kennel, if in an open covert, and hearing a pack of hounds in full cry near, I moved off in an opposite direction, but sometimes not without being seen by some of the wide and skirting hunters, who lost their day's sport in riding after me and hallooing "Tally-ho!" but I always kept quiet in my kennel when I heard hounds in full cry if I happened to be in a strong gorse-covert. Thus passed off the greater part of the first winter of my life.

On one occasion I was lying in rather an exposed place by the side of a pit, in the middle of a field, when I saw a man pass by on horseback, who, on seeing me, stopped, and after looking a short time, rode on. Till the noise of his horse's feet was out of hearing I listened, and then stole away, which was most fortunate, for in the course of a few hours the hounds were brought to the pit, the man having told the huntsman where he had seen me, as he thought, asleep; though we foxes, however it may seem, are seldom otherwise than wide awake.

When the month of February arrived, I showed my gallantry by going and visiting an interesting young friend of mine of the other sex in a large covert some distance off, and there, to my chagrin, I met no less than three rivals.

One morning we were surprised by hearing the voice of Foster, drawing the covert with his hounds, and giving his peculiar " E-dhoick! e-dhoick! kille-kid-hoick (probably for Eloo-in-hoick)!" It seems that none of us felt very comfortable or much at home here, and all must have left our kennel about the same time; for the hounds were soon divided into several packs and running in full cry in different directions. Fortunately, those that were following me were stopped; at which I rejoiced not a little, having travelled twenty miles the night before, besides my wanderings in and about the covert. These travellings and wanderings are the cause why so many more of us dog-foxes are killed by hounds in the month of February than in any other three months of the year. Two dog-foxes which had come from a great distance were killed by the hounds that day. I had had reason to be jealous of them, as they had for the last week or two been tracing and retracing the woods in pursuit of a female incessantly each night, until daylight appeared, when they were obliged through fatigue to retire to their kennels.

I recollect hearing, as I lay that day in a piece of thick gorse, the following proof of the patience and good temper of Sawyer, the whipper-in. The hounds had followed a fox into a wood close by, having hunted him some time in close pursuit, when a jovial sort of person, who constantly rode after these hounds, saw a fresh fox—being no other than myself — and began hallooing to the full extent of his voice. Sawyer immediately rode up to him, and addressed him thus: "Now, pray Mr. W——, don't ye halloo so, don't ye halloo; 'tis a fresh fox!" But still the person continued as loud as ever. The same entreaty was repeated again and again, and still he would halloo. At last Sawyer gave it up as a forlorn hope, and left him, just remarking, "Well, I never see'd such an uneasy creature as you be in all my life." He then followed the pack, which had by that time left the cover in pursuit of the first fox, which they had been running all the time. Yet we foxes have reason to know that a more determined and ardent enemy to us in the shape of a whipper-in than this man never lived. It fortunately happened for me that the weather now became very dry; for I was not unfrequently disturbed by these hounds, and though the scent was not very good in this plough country, I was at times much more distressed after being hunted than on former occasions, and was often nearly beaten; for it is not in our nature to be moving in the heat of the day, and not being so much inured to it as the hounds were, I expected to fall a prey to their able huntsman, who, when his hounds would not hunt me, appeared to know where I was gone to; and very often, when all was silent and I thought myself safe, brought them on without hunting, and crossing the line I had come; so that against him and his clever whipper-in, I had, notwithstanding the dry weather, enough to do to save my life.

On one occasion I had a most severe day's work, for the scent was remarkably good. I was lying quiet in my kennel, very unwilling to move, though I heard the hounds running a fox close to me, which they very soon lost, as they could not, or would not, hunt it. I thought this very strange, as by the use of my nose I knew it to be a good scenting day. It turned out that the fox was a vixen, which had just laid up her cubs; the effect of which generally is, that the scent becomes so different that hounds, old ones particularly, appear to know it, as if by intuition, and will not hunt it. As I had not had more notice of their approach I thought my best chance of escape was to be perfectly still,—a plan often adopted by me since on a good scenting day; but it was of no use, for the huntsman almost rode upon me in drawing the cover, and I was obliged to fly when the hounds were close to me; however, after a long run, I most luckily escaped.

The breeding season for game now came on, and being still young I frequently was near being tempted to seize an old bird as she sat on her eggs, but the difference in the scent of the bird prevented me. At length, when I had been prowling about near a farmyard in which poultry were kept, one night that I had not met with other food, I pounced on a hen which was sitting in a hedge, but the state she was in gave such an unpleasant taste to her flesh, that after eating a little I left it, and have never since touched a bird of any sort when sitting. She has at that time, indeed, but little flesh on her bones, and I believe that no old fox will take one for his own eating, although a female may sometimes carry one off, when hard pressed for food for her young. The same instinct which prevents hounds from hunting a fox with young, thus prevents much destruction of birds when sitting. It seems like a design of nature to save the race of birds that have their nests on the ground from being entirely destroyed by ourselves, or by vermin, such as stoats and weasels.

Rabbits are too often the perquisites of the gamekeeper, and the iron traps which he sets with the pretence of catching them are the destruction of hundreds of us. This might be prevented if the master would only insist on these traps not being employed at all, and compel the use of the wire snake, and of ferrets to get the rabbits out of their burrows.

Having by this time learnt from my mother all that she could teach me, I followed her example in many things. Amongst them I remarked, that on a wet and windy night she almost always chose, for various reasons, to lie in a gorse - covert. It is generally dry and without droppings from trees; it is also more quiet and freer from the roaring of the wind than when near to them. Besides this, we are not so liable to be disturbed by the shooters, and though we should be so, are out of sight. We are also there out of sight of some of our troublesome feathered neighbours, the crows, magpies, and jays, who would betray us when moving abroad during the daytime. They are always moving with the first appearance of daylight, and we are glad to get out of their sight as soon as we can and go into our kennel, lest they should betray us to the keepers, who are also often abroad at that time. The worst is, that at times, when we think we have got away from hounds which are hunting us, these birds, by making a noise and darting down almost upon us, as they continue to do where we run along, point out to the hunters exactly where we are.

It has often happened that I have been betrayed by an old cock pheasant. No bird has a quicker eye than he has, and directly he saw me he would begin kuckupping, and continue to make this noise as long as I remained near him, obliging me to move away.

My life during the summer months was one of almost uninterrupted pleasure. Naturally fixing my headquarters near the part of the country where I was bred, I would often ramble by night a great distance, and frequently remarked with surprise, as I crossed any line that I had taken when hunted, the wonderful straightness with which I had pursued it, as it was often in a direction where there were no large woods or earths; but I recollected that I had the wind for my only guide, and went as if blown forward by it; so that I could hear whether the hounds were following me at a greater distance than if I had gone against it; and besides this, it was more difficult for them to smell the scent which was lodged on the ground over which I had run, when blown away from their noses, than when blown towards them.

One circumstance occurred to check my joy, namely, the loss of my other brother, who had accompanied me in one of my midnight rambles into the adjoining country near Hambledon; and (for though so long ago as 1828, I well remember it) we had been induced to swim across some water to an island situated in Rookesbury Park, belonging to Mr. Garnier, on which it so happened there was a nest of young swans; and although we did not venture to touch them, the old ones were so angry with us for our intrusion, that when we attempted to quit the island they would not allow us to do so, but continued swimming backwards and forwards to show their anger. At length, as daylight was appearing, my poor brother was rash enough to make a sally, and had nearly swum across to the land, when, overtaking him, they commenced an attack, and by flapping their wings against his head, and keeping him under water, speedily drowned him, just as a man came up to see what they were about.

They seemed to exult in their prowess, and whilst they were proudly throwing back their heads, and rowing in triumph round their victim, I took an opportunity of crossing the water on another side and escaped, resolving never in swimming to encounter the same risk again. Nothing worth relating occurred until towards the beginning of the following winter. It is true that I was often induced to move and to quit the wood in which I lay, owing to my being disturbed by the hounds; but as they never followed me far, and were stopped by the whipper-in when I left the covert, it was evident they came on purpose to hunt young cubs; I therefore took care to retire to a gorse-covert near Sutton Common, where none were bred, much to the regret of the owner, a Rev. Baronet, who is one of our greatest friends, as no keeper of his would dare to destroy a fox without pain of losing his place. Here I remained quiet for some months, till one morning I was waked by the noise of Foster the huntsman; and shortly afterwards the whimpering of a hound told me that he was on the scent left by my footsteps on my way to my kennel, although it was where I had passed before day, and several hours had gone by. I was led by the wind that day to take them over a country seldom if ever gone over by them before, namely, Wolmer Forest, crossing one or two rivers, from extreme dread of this huntsman and his powerful pack. Whether it was the water or the fences that stopped him, I cannot say, but I suspect it was the latter; although a few years before nothing could have done it. The hounds were at times running without him, and it was in consequence of that, I think, that I eventually beat him and escaped. In the course of a few days I returned to the same covert, and had not been there more than fourteen more when this man's awful voice startled me again.

I was soon prepared for another run with a north-east wind, which might have led me to take the same line as before, but that I heard Sawyer the whipper-in exclaim, "'Tis our old fox, and he went through the same holes that he did the last time we found him." He gave the view-halloo directly afterwards. I felt certain that they came again thus soon determined if possible to kill me; and though frightened a little, I took care to keep on without stopping to listen, as I had done before; so that I kept a good distance ahead of them, and continued my best pace for many miles, crossing Wolmer Forest into Sussex. I no longer heard the hounds following me, and being much distressed with fatigue, ran forward to very short distances, and then turned either to the right or to the left, in order to baffle my pursuers. At length I came opposite to some buildings, and seeing a large pile of wood, crept in amongst it and lay down. After listening for some time, I heard the cry of a few hounds not far off; but the noise ceased just about the spot where I turned down the road, and all was silent for some time. At last I heard the voice of Sawyer the whipper-in, saying he must take the hounds home to the kennel if his horse would enable him; but that the huntsman's and the other whipper-in's horses were both done; and so they were, for they never lived to reach their stable.

Having again escaped from that clever huntsman Foster and his pack, I determined at first to remain in this part of Sussex. It was hunted by Colonel Wyndham, whose hounds I soon had reason to know were not less fatal than those by which I had lately been so severely hunted. They seemed to me to be quicker in their work, and to keep closer to me when it was a good scenting day; although when it happened to be otherwise they could not hunt me so long or so far as the other pack had done. Once or twice when I was nearly tired they left me, owing to the scent being bad, and went to find another fox, when I believe that Foster and his pack would have gone on longer, if not killed me. The pace they obliged me to go, when hunting me over the hills, was terribly fast, and very probably the cause of their not making so much cry when in pursuit. Indeed they ran almost mute, and at times got very near to me before I was aware of their approach.

This I found was too dangerous a country for me to remain in; and so, when on another occasion they found me, I ran into the Hambledon country, not far from Stanstead Forest, where I fortunately escaped, and finding myself in a wild part near Highdown Wood, did not venture to return, feeling sure that with the Colonel's quick pack and blood-like horses, if they found me on a good scenting day I must be beaten by them. However, here was in store for me as great a trial of my powers; for it seemed that Mr. Osbaldiston's hounds were just come for this part of the season to hunt the country. One morning I heard Sebright's voice cheering on his pack, which, with a burning scent, were running a fox like lightning. Suddenly there was an awful silence; then Dick Buxton's screech, and the "Whoop!" soon followed. For a minute or two only I heard a noise, as if hounds were quarrelling, and that no sooner ended than Sebright saying, "Now, Mr. Smith, this is the first real good scenting day we have had." I could stop no longer, but stole away, hoping not to be seen; but, my friends, fancy my horror when, on stealing from the gorse on the open down, and thinking that the rising ground would screen me, I saw this famed pack and first-rate huntsman within two hundred yards of me. I stopped for an instant, but scorned to return into the gorse, so took away across the hilly downs near Hog's Lodge, and crossed the Petersfield road to Portsmouth, over the open down for two miles, with the pack viewing me the whole time, except a moment or two when I was rounding the tops of the hills, then again they saw, and swung after me down the steep sides of the hills. I cleared the first fence adjoining the down, and had scarcely got fifty yards when I saw the whole pack flying over it after me, and at the next fence I turned short to the right as soon as I had cleared it. They were driven a little beyond it before they turned, which gave me a trifling advantage. I now continued to gain ground in advance of the pack, and though they never once were at fault, or lost the scent for a minute, and went on several miles across open downs into Sussex, still I kept on, determined to save my life.

I had gone full nine miles as straight as I could

go, and had just turned for the first time to the right, and was ascending the top of the highest point of the down, when, to my great joy, I saw the hounds stopping and trying in vain to recover the scent, which was destroyed by my having run through a large flock of sheep. They now could not hunt the scent a step farther, though on the middle of an open down; and such was the disappointment and chagrin occasioned by it to Sebright, that he was heard by a friend of mine to say, that if the squire would give him a thousand a year, he would not stop to hunt a country, where the scent was so soon entirely lost; and that, until this occurred, nothing in the world would have made him believe that any fox could have run straight away from such a pack as his, under such apparently favourable circumstances.

I remained till the following season in this part of the country, in a covert belonging to Sir J. Jervoise, called the Markwells, when I was first roused from my slumber by the voice of another huntsman, Mr. Smith,[1] who at that time hunted his own hounds, known as the Hambeldon pack. It was about one o'clock in the afternoon, in the month of December, and fortunately I prepared

[1] The author.—ED.

"Trying in vain to recover the scent."

myself for a day's work, for sure enough I had it. When I first broke covert I took the open, and in running had the wind in my face for about two miles, then finding the new pack pressing close to my heels, I turned short back with the wind, which, most fortunately, as it appeared to me, was now blowing in a direction straight to a large earth that I had formerly discovered at Grafham Hill in Sussex. The pace had blown the hounds, and the great change, by turning back and down the wind, caused them to stop for a minute or two; and although I soon heard them again hunting me, at a pace not quite so fast, their perseverance induced me to keep on straight forward. I had already gone for about ten or twelve miles, when, crossing a grass field near some buildings, I was startled at hearing the noise of other hounds close by. It was the pack in Colonel Wyndham's kennel. A view-halloo, which came from one of his men, made me continue to get on as fast as I could, and by the time it was nearly dark I fortunately reached the large earth at Grafham Hill. I had not been there for more than a few minutes when, lying with my head near the entrance of the earth in order to breathe more freely, I heard the hounds come up to the spot and try to get in, on which I retreated, but no farther than I was obliged to do, according to the plan I always adopted when distressed or nearly run down.

The distance I had run, straight ahead from where I started, was found to be twenty-seven miles. One of the four or five men who came in said that they must have changed their fox when the hounds ran through these large coverts. The reply was that it was scarcely possible, as they never once broke out of the road and rides, within which the fox had kept during the whole time.

It was now dark, and the hounds had full forty miles to return to their own kennel. I had reason, however, to know that they stopped that night half way, at the Drove Kennel; for during the night I had returned back as far as I could to the place whence I came, and intended to remain there; but all the middle of the next day I heard the sound of the horn which I had so often heard during the severe run I had had the day before, and which it appears was blown with the hope of its being heard by two hounds that were missed the night before, having come to the earth and remained some time after the pack had gone away. On hearing the horn I soon left my kennel, and, though very stiff, was obliged to make the best use of my legs that I could; for the pack, on their way home, crossed the line I had taken in the night, and were soon heard running in full cry after me. Glad was I to hear Mr. Smith order his men to stop them; for I must speedily have fallen to them had they only been aware of my weakness. One curious fact remains to be told, namely, that the two hounds remained for three days in the part near where they were left at the earth, and found their way back to the kennel on the fourth day afterwards. Now it is true that we foxes easily retrace our way on all occasions, but it must be recollected that we are often led straight by having in view some point, a main earth, for instance; when that is not the case, on being pursued by the hounds and guided by the wind, we notice the different points as we pass, and choose that line in which it appears least likely for us to be viewed; we thereby without difficulty retrace our line the same night, at least for some distance, unless too exhausted to travel more than necessary to procure food, when we remain near where the hounds have left us. I have done this for a short time, when the coverts and country to which I belonged have been much disturbed by the hounds; but invariably returned the same night. Now the hound has enough to do when hunting us without taking notice of the country which he passes over; and we must not assume to ourselves greater sagacity than belongs to him, for I believe that we are but varieties of the same kind. I observe amongst our party one who may have something to say upon that subject presently.

I underwent another severe day's work in the same country with another pack of hounds. In consequence of finding plenty of rabbits in a covert near the Waterloo Inn, I remained there for some time, and my peace was undisturbed, until I was roused one morning by the strange but fine voice of Mr. King's huntsman, Squire. After running round the covert a few times, I found that his quick pack were not to be trifled with; I therefore went straight away in the direction of Sussex. They still pressed me on through the large coverts there, and I left them in a wood, their huntsman and his master, Mr. King, imagining that I had gone to ground in a wood in Colonel Wyndham's country—a mistake which happened in consequence of my having crept into an earth that I remembered to have seen there, but which, when I found that it was merely a rabbit earth, I left, and went on. The hounds stopped there, but it was soon discovered that they would not lie, and the delay caused my escape, for I must otherwise have been killed. It was a terribly severe day, for I had been hunted by them more than twenty miles from the place where they found me. A great part of the country I ran across was the same that I had gone over in the previous year when hunted by Mr. Smith's pack, though the distance was not so far by some miles. The great difference I observed in these two packs was that the present one were rather faster, and could not be heard so plainly when running: this was in some measure made up for by Squire's voice, which I so often heard to cry "Whoop!"

I was afraid to remain in these parts, so travelled westward, until I reached a wood by the sea-side near Southampton, and there, owing to the scarcity of rabbits, was obliged to seek other food, often consisting of dead fish, which I found on the shore. I had more than once a narrow escape from being shot by sailors, as they passed by in a boat at moonlight, and was induced to leave this part also. Following the sea-shore I crossed the Itchen Bridge, for I had not forgotten my escape from the swans, and would never trust myself again in water when it could be avoided, and by degrees, as the spring came on, I got into the New Forest. Fortunately for me the system of hunting in that part until near the middle of May was discontinued by Mr. Codrington, who then hunted it. He was an excellent sportsman; and would never take an unfair advantage of us, but left all to his hounds.

Although I had escaped during the winter months from other good packs, it was doubtful that I could have escaped at this season, when the weather is sometimes very hot; for although, as I have observed before, the heat affects the hounds, it is more usual for them to be moving about in it than it is for us, and they therefore suffer from it less.

I passed this summer most agreeably, living much on beetles, with which the forest abounds, occasionally visiting the sea-shore to seek for dead fish, and getting a fair supply of rabbits. The old rabbits frequently laid up their young in the open parts of a country, in the middle of fields, or any where far from hedges, probably to be more out of the way of stoats and weasels. The number of nests of young rabbits that a single one of us destroys is so enormous that it would seem to many quite incredible. I got well acquainted with the purlieus of the forest in my frequent travels; in spite of which my feet were never tired by treading on hard flints, as they used to be in upper Hampshire; and, strange as it may appear, in that flinty country I do not recollect ever having had them cut or made sore by them, even when I was pursued by the hounds; probably in some measure owing to our quickness of sight, and to our not having to hunt a scent, so that our attention is not diverted. I believe I owed to these very flints the salvation of my life, as they obliged the hounds to go more slowly over them, and thus afforded me more time.

The autumn had nearly passed, and being undisturbed by hounds, I flattered myself that I was safe; but my dream soon vanished; for it appeared that the only reason why they had not disturbed me was, that they are not allowed to hunt in the forest so early as is done in other countries. I was soon alarmed by hearing at intervals Mr. Codrington's deep voice, so unlike the style of the huntsmen by whom I had been hunted in other parts. The hounds appeared to understand it well enough, and as they soon spread through the covert adjoining that where I lay, I stole away to some distance, where I remained within hearing of them. It was a long time before they left the first covert, as it happened to be one in which I had been moving about when searching for food, and consequently these well-nosed hounds got on my scent, there called "the drag." This fine old huntsman believing that a fox was near, persevered for an unusual length of time in trying to find one, and owing to one or two hounds occasionally throwing their tongues, waited in an agony of expectation. At length being led to the covert which I had just left, they soon got on the line which I had taken when I came from my kennel two hours before, and which they had great difficulty in hunting. By this time I thought it right to leave the wood where I had stopped. A man saw me go away, and hallooed loudly, but still the hounds were not allowed to be brought on; and they continued a walking pace until they got to the spot where I had waited, at the extremity of the wood, and where, though at some distance, I heard the cry of the hounds following me too closely to be despised by me as they had hitherto been. It seemed that they were left entirely to themselves, for I heard no men's voices cheering them on, as in other countries when running in the same way. As they continued without any stopping, I resorted to the only means then in my power, and ran through a herd of deer, with which the forest abounds. This plan succeeded, and probably saved my life; for when the deer heard the hounds coming towards them in full cry, they came straight after me in the line I had run, and so spoilt the scent which I had left.

I well recollect, a short time after this, overhearing, as I lay in my kennel, the following conversation between two men as they rode by : " What a pity it is that Mr. Codrington is so silent when his hounds are hunting their fox." " Well, I don't know that ; for suppose now you saw some weasels hunting a rabbit, do you think they would hunt it better if some fellow was to keep on hallooing to them?" No reply followed the question, although I anxiously waited to hear one. As far as I was concerned, I regretted that more noise was not made, as it would have assisted me, and not the hounds. The silent system is, at all events, a most dangerous one for the fox before he is found. I have had some narrow escapes from these very hounds being brought to a small covert or bog in this forest so silently that they surrounded me before I was aware, and I have with difficulty got away from them. Indeed, many female foxes have thus been killed heavy with cub, and in that state incapable of great exertion. Had these females heard the huntsman's voice in time they might have moved and run to earth, or shown in what state they were, so that the hounds might have been stopped in time to save their lives. As to the system of not assisting the hounds, I am sure that every fox will agree with me in approving it. Give me plenty of roads and dry fallows, or a few deer or sheep, and even when the scent is good I shall not fear to be killed by an unassisted pack. Without such impediments a pack so educated would be the most dangerous of all, and even with them, if in the hands of a judicious huntsman.

This pack was (alas! that I should say was, for he is no more,) hunted by a kind-hearted and excellent man, who has been heard to say, at a moment when his hounds were running very hard, and going like Leicestershire—he being nearly twenty stone—"I hope I shall not see them any more till they have killed." Notwithstanding the system just described, as many of my friends have fallen victims to this pack as to any in this part of the country. Nevertheless here I shall remain for the present, and not go away until I am fairly driven.

I now, my friends, conclude for the present the history of my life, only omitting such important events as may happen to come out in the course of your own stories; for I must now call upon you to tell us what you have to say of yourselves.

But hold hard there. Who or what art thou, half-bred thing, that durst be showing thy ill-breeding with feigning to sleep, or with eating rabbit, when thou shouldst have listened to the words of thy betters? Cock-tail, speak.

"Call me Cock-tail, half-bred, ill-bred, mongrel cur; but know that I claim kindred with your noble selves."

All. "Audacious dog-face!"

"Honour ye the Cock-tail! Cock-tail had a grandfather!"

All. "Impossible! Never!"

"Listen, then, to facts; facts are stubborn things, and if my story do not please, it may at least surprise you."

COCK-TAIL'S STORY

T is known, I believe, that half-bred animals do not reproduce their kind, and if it were otherwise innumerable would be such kinds. My mother's father was a fox. Her mother was a well-bred terrier in colour much like your own. She belonged to a man who lived near Harborough, in Leicestershire, and was valuable to him for her extraordinary talent in killing rats and mice, as well as for the use which he occasionally made of her in poaching at night. Wishing to procure a mixed breed between her and a fox, he took her one night, at a particular period of the spring, to a certain spot in a wood which he knew to be much frequented by foxes, and having fastened her against a tree, left her there till morning. On the following night he removed her to a short distance from the spot where she was left the night before. After doing the same for several nights he took her home, and in nine weeks after that she produced four young ones, all of which are now living, and much like a fox. My father was a brown terrier, and my mother may be seen at any time, as she is fastened up by a chain in the inn-yard at Market Harborough. The hair on her back and sides is thick, and stands nearly upright like that of a fox. The hairs upon the upper side of the tail are not so long and full as those of a fox, but the under part and the sides are the same; the tips of them are black. Her legs and feet are black, and the latter are round like yours, with a little tan-colour behind the knee-joint. Her ears are pointed, and when she is at rest laid back, but when she is roused pricked up like your own. All these properties you may behold in me, but not exactly in an equal degree. The most remarkable difference between ourselves and you is this, that neither my mother nor myself are endued with the strong odour peculiar to the fox. My mother has never been let loose by the consent of her keepers, even in the inn-yard; but having once got loose by accident, when about two years old, she ran away a long distance, and being followed into a yard was there secured again. It was observed when running that she carried her tail level as I do, like a fox; sometimes it was crooked, but never upright. It was not so much curled as mine is.

I lived with my mother, and when I was two years old, a master of fox-hounds happening to hear of us, came to see us; and after making many inquiries, persuaded my owner to let him take me away with him. I was then placed under the care of the old feeder of hounds, with orders that I should be allowed to run about in the house, with his children for companions. I was shown to every one as a curious animal, and became a great favourite, but all attempts to tame me failed, and I never would let a stranger touch me. My master took me out with his dogs when he went to shoot rabbits, but found me wholly useless. The sound of the gun and the barking of the dogs frightened me so much that I always ran away into the nearest hedge or wood to hide myself; and I felt that my fate was sealed when I heard the old feeder say to my master one day, "Now, sir, I am sure that this here 'vulp'" (for so I was called) "will never be no use at all; for he is as wild and timorous now he is two years old as ever he was. We can't get un to do anything like the terriers; he frisks about like an eel, so as we can't touch un at times." Finding that I had no friend to say a good word for me I absconded, and when seen at a distance have often been mistaken for a fox, and scared by the cry of "Tally-ho! tally-ho!" and the hounds following me. That they never caught me I suppose may be attributed to my not having the fox's strong scent.

"Thy story is marvellous; but I must doubt its truth until I see thy mother. I fear that thou art like other vain creatures, who, knowing their own unworthiness, would fain connect themselves with those who are in any way excellent, but beware of betraying us."

"Ha! is it so? I am off."

"He is gone, and grins defiance! This mongrel will think nothing of destroying us by the dozen; but he may suffer for it yet.

"And now, my friends, as we have heard the mongrel's account of himself, let us hear Craven's story. Open thy lips and throw thy tongue freely; tell us how many times thou hast beaten these vexatious hounds, and be not chary of thy experience."

CRAVEN'S STORY

IT is unnecessary to enter into the ordinary details of my life after having heard our friend who invited us here. Consequently my story will be a short one. I was born and bred in Savernake Forest, in the Craven Hunt, where my father and mother had been considered to be of some importance, having often beaten a famous pack of hounds in that country. To the best of my recollection, the first pack of hounds by which I was hunted belonged to Mr. I. Ward; from them I had many narrow escapes, which I now, having since been hunted by other hounds, set down to their immense size, for although they could and did hunt me in an extraordinary manner, and pursued me closely in the flat country and in the forest, yet I found that I left them far behind when running over the flinty hills which separate that country from Mr. Ashton Smith's. Their steady style of hunting made it difficult to shake them off elsewhere. I once overheard a man remark to their master that they were larger than any that he had ever seen, especially as to their heads. The reply at first surprised me. "Yes, I like them large, for when once they get them down in hunting they are so heavy that they cannot get them up again." After being hunted by them under his direction, I was hunted by them when they belonged to Mr. Horlock, from whom also I have had some narrow escapes, principally by running through large woods, where they soon changed me for another fox. I recollect once, when lying in a small covert near Benham Park, I was startled by hearing the cry of another but smaller pack of hounds, as I could distinguish them to be by the sound of their tongues. Shortly afterwards I saw a fox pass near me much distressed, and very soon the fatal "whoop" was heard. It afterwards appeared that this gentleman's brother had permission to try whether he could kill with his small pack a fox which had more than once beaten the large one. The following season I was surprised one morning by hearing the voices of some different men with hounds, drawing the wood in which I lay. I soon moved and went away from the wood, but was seen by men, who commenced hallooing, "Gone away!" The hounds were then hunting another fox in the wood, where they continued all day without killing him. At length I was found by them where there was no other fox. They pursued me for many miles in a most extraordinary way, and such good hunting hounds they were, that had I not gone down a road where a flock of sheep had just gone before, unknown to the huntsmen, I must have been killed. They there came to a check, and as it was contrary to Mr. Wyndham's system to assist his hounds by holding them forward, they never got near me again that day. It was very like the system described by our friend in the New Forest.

The following year I was again surprised by hearing the voice of another strange huntsman, before I knew that hounds were just coming into the wood. However, this notice was sufficient to prepare me for a start. Soon after I had moved from my kennel, a single hound threw his tongue. Mr. Smith gave a very loud cheer, and every

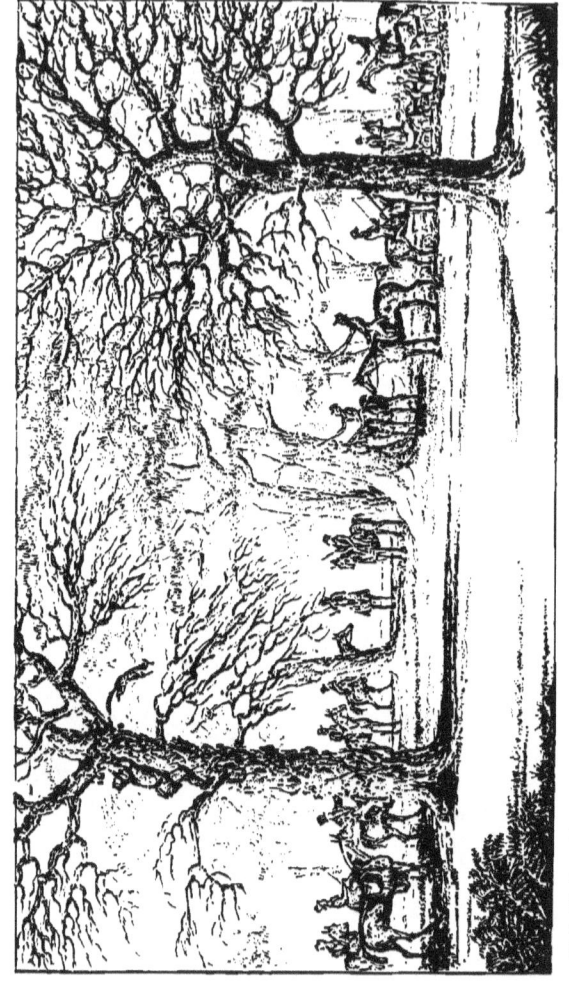

T. Smith, Esq., del.

THE CRAVEN HOUNDS IN SAVERNAKE FOREST.

Fox 27 feet from the ground.

Facing page 65.

hound appeared at once to be running on the scent. This so frightened me that I lost no time in leaving the covert and taking my way straight to the forest, where other foxes were soon moved by hearing the hounds; I escaped this time also. Not feeling however quite safe, I resorted to a plan which had been adopted by other foxes before. I contrived to crawl up the side of a large oak tree, by means of some small branches which grew out of its trunk near the bottom, and the stems of ivy which covered it farther up. At a considerable distance from the ground I found a desirable spot to rest upon, where the large branches, about which was a thick patch of the ivy, divided. To this place I resorted every morning for a long time, and thence could frequently see the horrible hounds, myself lying, as I fancied, in certain safety. One day, however, as I turned my head towards where they were hunting a fox in the wood close by, my attention was so riveted that I did not observe a keeper, who in passing the tree on the other side had seen me and was proceeding towards the hounds just at the moment the fatal "whoop!" was heard,—the hounds having killed the unfortunate fox which they had been hunting.

Soon afterwards the keeper told Lady Elizabeth

Bruce where I was; it was also communicated to Mr. Smith, who said, that although the hounds had had a hard day's work, the fox should be dislodged from his extraordinary situation if her ladyship wished to see it done. To my horror, the keeper brought the hounds straight to my tree and pointed to the spot where I lay as close as I could. As soon as they were taken away to a considerable distance and out of sight, the keeper was desired to climb up the tree and bring me down. The horror of my situation may be easily conceived as I heard him ascending. I did not move until I saw his hand close to me; but as he was on the point of taking hold of me I sprang from my lofty nest. Fortunately dropping on some branches which projected about half way down, I broke the fall, which would have broken my neck, and fell to the ground, from which I rebounded, I think, some feet. Much shaken by the fall, but fortunately nothing worse, I soon was on my legs and away across the forest straight to the west woods, which were about three miles distant. When the hounds were only the distance of half a field they saw me enter this immense covert; but, as several foxes were soon moving, I escaped; and the hounds were kept running till it was nearly dark. I have since heard that the height from which I sprang to the ground was afterwards measured to decide a bet, and that it was proved to be exactly twenty-seven feet. It was a strange adventure, but can be attested by many who saw it; and with this I conclude my story.

Now for Northampton Pytchly. Thou art familiar with these things; thou hast, no doubt, thy story by heart, and canst go a slapping pace.

PYTCHLY'S STORY

RECOLLECT that when the pace is good it cannot last long, and so with my story, for I remember but little of my very early days. I have had the good luck to escape from several packs of hounds which have hunted my country, and am now arrived at a venerable age; indeed, so far advanced in my teens that I began to believe myself to be the oldest fox in the country, until I saw one who is fastened up by a chain in the back-yard of the Peacock Inn, at Kettering. Having been there ever since he was a cub, he is known to be eighteen years old, and he is now full one-fourth shorter than when in his prime of life. It is not likely that foxes often attain to such an age, as before that they become infirm;

and in countries where there are hounds become an easy prey to them, and where there are no hounds they are killed by the gamekeepers.

The first pack of hounds by which I was hunted belonged to Mr. Osbaldiston, and a most trimming pack they were; but luckily for me, when they were going their best pace in pursuit of me, they sometimes overran the scent, owing to their great courage, which, in the breeding of them, seemed to have been more attended to than the nose. They sometimes ran away for a little while even from all the fast riders. These, however, generally contrived to get up again to them, especially when at a check; but every moment's delay made more clear to all the necessity of having best noses.

It may appear strange that I should have escaped from the different packs, since the Squire's[1] left, in so fine a country as this to which I belong, especially when such expense has been incurred to procure a strong pack on purpose to destroy us; but, luckily for us, the hunters fell into the mistake of trying to make what they called a flying pack, and to this end getting rid of all those which they called slow hounds, many of which were such as would not

---

[1] To Mr. Osbaldiston belonged, *par excellence*, the title of "the Squire."—ED.

go the pace without a good scent, as they would have them do. Such hounds were always drafted, although, when there was a good scent, this sort could puzzle even the fast riders to keep with them. Partly to this cause, then, I attribute my having lived to my great age. There are other reasons why fewer foxes are killed than formerly. In the first place, the country is overrun with drains, of which there are thousands unknown to the hunters, but known to us. When severely pressed by the hounds, I have often got into one of them, and it frequently happened to be in the middle of an open field, when hounds in chase of me have run over it; and owing to their mettle and to their being pressed by hard riders, they have been urged on beyond it, then held on forward in every way by the huntsman; and if, after this, the drain has been discovered, the scent, owing to the time lost, has been nearly gone. The entrance to drains is generally in a low part of the land, which is chilled by water upon it, and therefore may not hold a scent to discover that we have gone into one.

During the time that that fine old sportsman, Lord Spencer, hunted this country, there were nothing like so many of these drains as there are now, which may in some measure account for fewer foxes being killed at the present time than when Charles King hunted the hounds. I have heard my old granny say that the first thing his lordship thought of and wished to do, was to improve and strengthen his pack in every possible way. Of late, the pack has been thought to be of least consideration; and it would seem by the system adopted, that a fox is to be run down by men who can ride fast, and that whippers-in are nearly all that is wanted. For instance, when I have been pursued by the hounds, if I have run towards or through any covert, I have frequently been astonished, after passing through it, and almost before the hounds had arrived at it, to see one of the whippers-in riding beyond it, in order to see me go away, which he rarely or never could do; and if he did by accident get in time to see me at all, the consequence was, that when I saw him I went back again into the covert, and then, if there was any fresh fox or foxes in it, they were pretty sure to be changed and hunted, and I escaped. It generally happened that I had gone on through the covert before the whipper-in got round, in time to see, not me, but a fresh fox go away, to which he would probably halloo on the hounds, and, not knowing the difference, declare it was the hunted one.

I suppose you will now not wonder that I have lived to so great an age in this country. It is true I have had some narrow escapes within the last few seasons, particularly one in the year 1840, when I was found by the hounds then belonging to Mr. Smith, and in consequence of beating them, called the Hero of Waterloo. I attributed my escape to the system above described and adopted by the men on that occasion, when the hounds were hallooed on to a fresh fox, which the whipper-in Jones had viewed away on the farther side of Loalland Wood, at a time when the hounds were hunting my scent through it, I having gone through and away from it long before he got there. On looking back I witnessed, to my regret, Mr. Smith's displeasure at the system, which from that time he insisted should not be continued. However, I was, four days afterwards, lying in a small wood at Kelmarsh, when the hounds pursued a fox in full cry, and came straight towards where I lay. Just before they arrived I heard the following words addressed by Mr. Smith to his whipper-in: "Where are you riding to before the hounds, when they are running hard? Keep behind them in your place. If we cannot kill our fox without your acting thus, we had better have a pack of whippers-in, and no hounds at all." I never heard of or saw the same system again.

Many other changes took place, which, as being unlike what we had been used to, were by no means agreeable to us. One of them was the former way of giving up hunting a fox and going to find another. On some occasions, when I have been found and hunted by the hounds, and fancied that I was safe, as I had done on previous occasions whenever I could not hear them, I was surprised to hear them, after a short time, again hunting on the line I had come. I was once found by the hounds in a covert close to Fox Hall, and after they had pursued me closely for a few miles, I, in consequence of there being a line of dry fallows, left them far behind; so that I had given up all idea of being disturbed again by them that day, and stopped in Mr. Hope's plantation; I had been but a short time there when they again approached, but slowly, and I heard the following words addressed to Mr. Smith, who was hunting his hounds: "How much longer shall you go on with this cold scent? Don't you think you can find another fox?" The reply was, "I shall hunt this as long as a hound will own the scent. We shall get up to him by and by, and kill him too."

On hearing this it was time to be off. I was

shortly after seen in the plantation, and hunted closely by the hounds, which, after another long check, again got on my scent in the wood where I was *first found*. They hunted me very fast across some of the finest grass country, and I was obliged to take refuge in a drain under a road leading to a field, where fortunately I found another fox, and succeeded in getting beyond him in his retreat. It often occurs that the fox which is hunted and frightened forces his way beyond the fresh one, and there remains during the operation of digging, and when the huntsmen come by, the fresh fox is drawn out and given to the hounds. Such was the case now, and so I escaped, for luckily it was getting late, and the hounds were taken away immediately without their discovering that I was left behind. I had time to remark that only one man, who was addressed as his Grace, was with the hounds at the finish, or indeed for a long time during the run, nearly all having left at the time of slow-hunting.

And now, my friends, I have done.

"Done! Tell us first what has become of our friend old King Stumpy. There is a rumour that he is dead, and I do not perceive any one here without a brush."

Alas! he is no more. He was captured, and

massacred, and died an ignominious death. It happened last autumn that he was found as usual in Grafton Park one morning, as soon as it was light, by this new pack, when he had imprudently glutted himself, and was thinking again to save his life by immediately running into a drain, in which he had so often saved himself before after a severe day's hunting. He who had been king of the forest, and had for so many years fairly beaten his enemies, was now dug out and devoured by the hounds on the spot. Oh! the ruthless and unfeeling beasts! Yet, be it confessed, that we ourselves do sometimes dig out a mouse or so, but it is to eat him kindly, you know.

Here I intended to finish my story, but as I am expected to explain how I have escaped from every pack by which I have been hunted, I must add, that having for a long time had a wish to see that part of the Northampton country hunted till last year by the Duke of Grafton's hounds, in which the woods were of immense size, having heard that T. Carter and his killing pack had left the country, and thinking it would be a place of greater security for my old age, I went there last spring, but had not been long settled in Puckland's woods before I was disturbed by hearing another pack, which soon found me out, and pursued me for some time most closely, till at length they came to a check. When listening, I heard a person ride up and use these words to the huntsman : " Well, what are you going to do now ? You had better be doing something ; it's no use standing still." There was some reply which I could not hear. However, I discovered that the man addressed was Taylor the huntsman, and that the pack was the remainder of that by which I had first been hunted when it belonged to Mr. Osbaldiston. The only difference I could observe was, that they were not quite so powerful. That they were stout enough I had reason to know; for although I escaped after their hunting me for several hours in these large woods, they afterwards killed another fox without leaving the covert.

On another day, when I was lying in a large covert adjoining the Forest of Whittlebury, and the hounds had been drawing some distance beyond the spot where I lay, I thought that I could steal away unseen, and had nearly reached the outside of the wood when I was much annoyed by the noise of a jay, which kept flying above me as I went on. When I stopped I heard a man say, "There is a fox moving close to that jay, I'll be sworn ; just look, you will see him cross that path directly."

This talking frightened me from the spot, and on my going a little farther and crossing a path, another man exclaimed, "There he goes! it was a fox that jay was making such a noise about." He then gave a loud view-halloo; the hounds soon came up, and after running some time in the forest, I left them following another fox.

The little I had to say is said.

"Come, Dorset, fain would we hear thy story next. Our thoughts should be open as the heavens above, and free as the winds that follow us. We are brethren and fellows in our way of life, and thou may'st not doubt that we will judge thy deeds fairly but kindly."

"Justice, then, is fled to lowly beasts, for men have none of it. Listen to my story, friends; a plain and unvarnished one it is, and you shall have it freely and entirely."

DORSET'S STORY

WAS born in Cranborne Chace, which is in Mr. Farquharson's hunt, and it was here that I first heard the sound of a huntsman's voice, the voice of old Ben Jennings; and melodious as it might have been considered by others, it was any thing but agreeable to my ear when he used it to cheer on his hounds, which appeared so well to understand it. It frequently was the cause of my leaving this large covert. I returned to it because the hounds were apt to get on the scent of another fox. The voice became at last so familiar to me that I heeded it not, but rather found amusement in it, taking little trouble to be out of hearing of it when the hounds were hunting me; but another season came, and great was the difference. I lay in a favourite covert called Short Wood, when I was startled by another voice instead of old Ben's, that of the new huntsman, Treadwell's, clear and beautiful—not so powerful as that which I had been used to of late, nor was it *vox et præterea nihil;* for his system was one which soon made me give up listening when the hounds were pursuing. I found that I had now no longer time to wait and hang about as I had done. I was obliged to get away as fast as I could, and had enough to do to escape from the new man, whose coolness and perseverance frightened me. My first escape was owing to an imperfect cast which he made when the hounds had come to a check in a field, where there was a flock of sheep, for instead of taking the hounds entirely round and close under the hedge, beginning at the left hand, he missed that corner for about fifty yards, where it happened that I had gone through the fence, and by the time he had taken them close all round every where else and held them on forward, time was lost, and the hounds got on the scent exactly opposite. Although it now became slow hunting, I did not feel safe until I heard him blow his horn to go home. I believe that this kind of mistake, or rather neglect, has been frequent on the part of other huntsmen by whom I have been hunted. Be that as it may, one or two escapes from this able man and his pack were sufficient to induce me to get quickly into another hunt out of his way. Those escapes may be attributed to the want of scent, and they will not seem surprising, if the time be calculated which was lost at every check, whilst I was going on without listening as the hare always does. Having stopped some little time in a strong covert of gorse in an open down, in Mr. Drax's country, south of Blandford, and close adjoining to Lord Portman's, I was one morning annoyed by hearing the voice of Mr. Drax's huntsman, John Last, who was drawing the covert with his hounds, by which I was shortly after surrounded. Being ignorant of the runs and tracks in the gorse, I was so pressed by them that I sprung upon the top of the gorse, and ran along it for a few yards, but the hallooing of the hunters soon frightened me down again. At length I went straight away across the down in view of all the hunters, and had not gone more than a hundred yards before a large man on a heavy gray horse rode between me and the covert, and began hallooing in the most frightful manner, at the same time waving his hat as if he was out of his mind; the consequence of which was, that the hounds, which were hunting me closely out of the covert, immediately they saw and heard him threw up their heads and ran wildly after him, expecting to see me, which fortunately they did not, as I had by that time just got beyond a small elevation in the down, which prevented the man also from seeing me. I turned directly to the left. He now found out the mischief he had done by causing the hounds to lift their heads, and galloped on still farther, hoping to get another view of me, but in vain, as I had sunk into a small valley, and he luckily turned the hounds in a direction opposite to that in which I had gone. The scene at this time defies description. "What are you at, you crazy old man? You have lost our fox!" and endless execrations were lavished on him. I believe this circumstance saved my life; for had it not occurred, the hounds would have had me in view for three miles across the downs, and although it was some little time before they got on my scent again, they came after me at a most terrific pace, which fortunately, however, was slackened on their crossing the road and having to climb over a wall into the grounds adjoining some immense woods, through the whole of which they hunted me again at a good pace, and straight on for nine or ten miles, till I was almost exhausted; luckily they were stopped when crossing a field where there was a flock of sheep, no one being there to assist them. Shortly I heard in a loud voice, "John! Where is John?" and finding that they were not likely to get much assistance from the huntsman, I quietly retraced my steps towards the place from which I started, but remained there for a short time only.

I was again lying one morning in a piece of gorse near the Down House, when I was waked by hearing what I thought was the whistle of the keeper, but which turned out to be that of Lord Portman's huntsman, whose hounds were all around me before I was aware. The men on horseback were scattered in all directions over the down, and it would have served them right if they had lost their day's sport, which they very nearly did, as I stole away to a large rabbit earth close by, into which I ran.

Unluckily some of the hounds got on my scent and hunted it up to the earth, where they marked it by stopping and baying. Shortly after this two or three of the hunters rode up, and I heard the following words: "Not worth saving: get him out and give him to the hounds; he can't run a yard." However, it was decided that I should have a chance, as they called it; and a pretty chance it was. I was dug out, put into a sack, and given to the whipper-in, with orders to turn me out on the down. Something was said about cutting my hamstrings, in order to lame me, and one wished to cut off my brush; and that it was not done was a great disappointment to the wretch. I was turned out at only about a hundred yards from the pack, but contrived to reach a hedge just as one of the leading hounds had got close to me, when I turned short to the left down the narrow ditch. The hounds all sprang over the fence, and then, not seeing me there, fortunately turned first to the right; and before they had found out that I had gone down the ditch I had got out on the other side again, and ran to a corner, when I turned through it again into another cross-hedge. By these means I got clear off before they had another sight of me, for they overran my line of scent a little when they got back on the down on my track. I well recollect hearing the huntsman calling loudly to the whipper-in to get on and head the fox from going to the woods; but he, poor thing, was in a state of too much excitement to understand what was meant, and even if he had understood, it would have been a fruitless attempt to stop me from making my point to reach a wood or place of safety on such an occasion, even if my first attempts had been prevented. I may flatter myself that a hundred witnesses are ready to pronounce it as clever an escape as was ever effected by a fox in similar circumstances. For the future they will not say that a fox cannot run, and condemn him to be given to the hounds, merely for running into an earth.

I now made the best of my way straight to the large woods which I had passed through when hunted by the other pack, and luckily made good use of my time, for they came after me as if their feet had been winged, neither road nor wall delaying them. I had enough to do to keep out of their way through these large woods, which they traversed nearly as fast as if in the open country. At the extremity of the woods, to my surprise, I met the noble master of the pack, who had succeeded in getting to that point before me, the result of which was that I turned back into the covert before he saw me, and caused a slight check, after which they again approached me, just as I had reached the wall which surrounded the wood, at the top of the hill looking into the vale, where I descended, and looking back saw the hounds for a short time again at a check, owing to that high ground being slightly covered with snow. I dreaded lest they should take the hounds on beyond the snow towards the vale where I was; but they soon turned back, and I heard no more. It was nearly three o'clock, which some think time to go homeward rather than from home, as would have been the case if they had followed me, when probably I should not have lived to tell my tale. The scent in the vale is always so much greater than on the hills from which they had hunted me, that I must have fallen a prey to this pack. Although we are endowed with so large a share of wisdom, it is not all-sufficient; or else we should be aware that when pursued by hounds and nearly beaten by them, it must be all but certain death to us to run from a bad scenting country into a good one.

Having now openly defeated the enemies who had conspired against me, I remained in the vale until I was tempted to move into a finer and fairer country. Great changes are going on in the hunting of the country which I left; and should we ever meet again there may be much for me to tell. For the present I have done.

"We now look to thee, Warwick, to give us something good; thy country has produced one of the most extraordinary men that ever lived. He knew all the wiles of the wiliest creature that walks the earth. Dost thou think that Shakespeare would have been a good huntsman?"

"By the faith of a fox I should have been most loath to try him. Did he possess the following qualities: boldness, perseverance, activity, enterprise, temper, and decision? Had he a keen perception of relative place? Had he a good eye and ear? If he had all these, and more, then might Shakespeare have been an immortal foxhunter.

"It is little that I have seen in this country, and I have little to tell; but I will at once proceed and state to what cause I attribute my escape on one or two occasions lately."

WARWICK'S STORY

N the month of March last I was lying in a strong gorse-covert, not far from Nuneham, when after hearing the voice of Stephens, the huntsman to the Atherstone[1] hounds, I heard the following remarks by one sportsman to another, both being on horseback and waiting close to where I was in my kennel.

"Well, I do hate that silent system; had Robert not been so sparing of his voice, or had he only given one blast of his horn when he began drawing the small spinney just now, the hounds

---

[1] Stephens was huntsman of the Warwickshire, not the Atherstone, pack.—Ed.

would not have chopped that vixen in cub; for vixens in that state are unable to run far, and are unapt to move till pressed to do so by the approach of danger. She probably had been so much used to see the keeper and his dogs pass, that, not hearing the huntsman's voice or horn, she was taken by surprise when the hounds got round her; if she had moved before, she might have been seen, and the hounds stopped in time to save her. No doubt she had been there some weeks before, and, in consequence of having a good friend at the great house not being ever disturbed, she believed that she was safe."

I would not venture to listen any longer, for I heard the same hounds running another fox in the gorse close by me. It appeared that there was also another besides, making altogether three of us. Finding this to be the case, and thinking to be very cunning, I took an early opportunity of quitting the covert; and had scarcely got across two fields before I saw a multitude of men on horseback riding along the road in a parallel direction to that which I was going. They had seen me leave the covert without waiting for the hounds, which they ought to have known were running still after another fox; however, when they found that the hounds were not running after the same fox that they were themselves, they began hallooing, and the hounds were shortly afterwards brought and got on my scent. Of course I returned to the covert, for I had no notion of being thus hunted by men, and wished to let the gentlemen know that I would not go unless I chose to do so, let them halloo as they would. I therefore punished them by running for nearly three quarters of an hour longer in the covert. This brought them a little to their senses, and they gave me room to make another attempt. Not liking to remain in such close quarters with this sticking pack, I seized an opportunity, and went away on the side of the covert opposite to that which I had first attempted, and though I was viewed away by several men, it happened that they were able this time to hold their horses and their tongues until I had got fairly away, when they certainly did halloo, so that about half the pack came to them. The whipper-in was sent to stop them, and as soon as the huntsman had got a few more he also came to them; but not having quite three parts of the pack he did not go on with them, but stopped and blew his horn for the others which he had left. Some of them shortly after came, but seeing him stopping where he was, did not appear to be in any haste, possibly because they were aware that they had left a fox in the covert; but, from his stopping, it might not have appeared to them that a fox had gone on, or they would not have taken it so leisurely.

To this, then, do I attribute my escape; for, though they did hunt me for a mile or so, the time was lost, and so too, of course, the scent; this, added to the impatience shown by the men who were out, settled the business for me. An accident which had lately occurred to Stephen, the huntsman, by which his foot was injured, prevented him, I conclude, from being every moment close to the hounds, when these men were so anxious to get on, and the huntsman's presence was so absolutely necessary to prevent their doing mischief. However, I had no reason to regret it, for I went straight across a fine country; though it was reported that I had returned to the covert, which was not likely; I may add, on this occasion, that I went to the coverts at Comb, to which place they also came to find another fox. They did not cross the line I had come, but passed through part of a large covert where I had stopped, without drawing it, expecting to find a fox at the other end of it.

Seeing this, I slipped back behind them, and was stealing away, as I thought undiscovered (no uncommon thing for me to do), but, unluckily, a man in a red coat had stopped back, as if on purpose to see any fox that might be left behind; and as soon as I was out of sight he gave a loud view-halloo, by repeating which he brought the hounds after a short time on to the line of my scent. This caused me to lose no time, and having now a good start, I ran straight through all those large woods until I got to the end of that near the railway, when I turned to the right; and after stopping in an outside covert for some time, thinking that I had escaped, I heard the hounds hunting very slowly, till they were quite silent. But I was soon after surprised to hear the huntsman taking them across the wood where I was, and instantly left it in a direction opposite to that where I had seen all the hunters ride; consequently only a few followed with the hounds when they hunted me across the river and railway into the open, beyond Coventry. They ran me back to near the side of the river, when they were taken to the other side, which happening to be towards Leamington, I remained in that part, and had got so far as Ufton Wood. I was found there a few days afterwards by the new huntsman of the Warwickshire hounds and that pack. Having previously heard that they had learned much from Carter, the

Duke of Grafton's late huntsman, under whom he had been whipper-in, and that he had been doing much mischief amongst us, I lost no time in leaving this large covert, and was soon followed by the pack, which hunted me at a fair pace, until they had followed me part of the way across a dry fallow field. As my good luck would have it, there was also another fallow in the direction which I had gone, straight beyond. It seems that Stephen, the huntsman, made one or two casts with his hounds across each of these fallow fields without success. In his anxiety not to lose, I suppose he forgot that if the hounds could not hunt scent over one fallow they could not over another. He omitted to hold the hounds on and across the next field of wheat beyond it, and took them back towards the covert where I came from, and thus it was that I escaped; for after some remark was made to him on the subject, he directly took the hounds back to the field beyond the fallow; they there got on my line of scent, and after hunting slowly for a couple of miles, fortunately for me gave it up; otherwise, the line I had taken was so good that I might have fallen a victim to this persevering and promising young huntsman. After a little more experience he will be a dangerous enemy of ours.

"Now, Chester, tell us how they go on in thy part of the world, and how thou hast contrived to escape from that famous hunting pack of hounds, which we are told belonged to the late Mr. Codrington. Tell us, moreover, is it a good huntsman they have to hunt them?"

CHESTER'S STORY

AS foxes are scarce in our country, I alone could be found to travel here, and having been hunted only one season, I am, from my own experience, but ill qualified to reply to your question as to the huntsman. I have as yet escaped from being hunted by him, but I do hear that he is in all respects most excellent. Unfortunately for him, but fortunately for us, he was lately disabled by the fracture of a bone of his leg; and consequently could not come with the hounds when they hunted the last week in the Namptwich country. For reasons to be given hereafter, I had rarely lain in coverts of late, and had preferred lying in hedgerows. I happened, however, to be lying in a covert one day when I heard the voice of a man who was hunting hounds which turned out to be Mr. White's, and as they were close to me before I heard them, my only chance was to leave the covert immediately; but in the first field I was met by some men on horseback who frightened me back again. I was not seen by the hounds, which ran out of the wood on my scent as far as I had gone, but were turned back, not without a little loss of time, which was a favourable occurrence for me. I went straight through the wood and away on the opposite side, and soon found that they were after me. I kept on, but not in a straight line, which rather puzzled the gentleman who was hunting them. They came at length to a final check, and could hunt no farther. I thought that if Marden had been hunting them, there was one cast which he would have made, and that was to the left of the field where they lost the scent; for although each of the other sides were tried by casting the hounds that way twice over, they were never taken once round beyond the field to the left; and to this I attribute by escape, for I was nearly beaten, and it appeared that the pack which I found such difficulty in shaking off and defeating by turning so short as I had done during the run, was that which belonged to the late Mr. Codrington. It is stated that they killed every fox that they hunted during eight following weeks. They are said not to be compared for beauty to the former pack, which is reported to have been a magnificent one; but "handsome is that handsome does."

Now, my friends, I will tell you why I prefer hedgerows and out-of-the-way places to fix on for a kennel. Listen to a matter of fact, but a melancholy story of what took place in a part of the country where I was bred. It happened when in a favourite little covert near Namptwich that I was attracted by the scent of a bait which was placed under a large iron trap, carefully covered over with some light grass and moss; on attempting to remove these I unfortunately struck the trap, which went off and caught me by the foot. Need I describe the agony I endured, confined as I was by the mangled foot? Daylight appeared, when, nearly exhausted with pain, I made a desperate effort with my other forefoot, and succeeded in pulling out the peg that confined to the ground the chain of the trap, which I dragged away for some distance, I then lay down overcome with pain, and in this deplorable condition remained for two or three days and nights. The foot being now as it were benumbed and almost insensible, I in order to save my life fairly bit it off with my teeth, and thus released myself from the trap. Not long after this had occurred a more tragical affair took place in this very same covert. In the early part of the month of March in the present year 1843, I was lying, as was my custom, in a thick and broad hedge, when late in the day I was much frightened by the approach of the hounds, passing near me rather quickly to my great relief, for it appeared that they had not found a fox all day. They immediately begun drawing the covert, and shortly afterwards a fox was seen with an iron trap fast to his foreleg, which was broken above the knee. In the course of a few minutes the fatal "whoop" was heard, the signal of his death.

During the tumult which ensued amongst the gentlemen who had been hunting, an honest farmer, whose land surrounded the covert, came up and stated that a short time before he had found in a field close by a large trap exactly of the same sort, which had in it two of a fox's toes. They belonged to the foot which I parted with myself. It is impossible to describe the sensation created by this additional circumstance; but it caused amongst other remarks the following, which reached my ears:—"These acts of shocking cruelty were scarcely ever heard of in this part, till game became an article of traffic to the landlord, and shooting on his land began to be let to strangers who have no interest whatever in the welfare of the country where it lies. Nothing conduces to that welfare more than brilliant sport afforded by a pack of hounds; as it leads others, as well as those who own estates, to become residents in the country. Noblemen and gentlemen have now lost their good old English feelings, and instead of inviting their friends for the sport, they let their shooting, or sell their game in the market. It frequently happens that the persons to whom the shooting is let are men who are engaged in business and reside in large towns. They are consequently ignorant of the tricks and cruelties of their keepers during their absence, and unaware of the disappointment these keepers create to hundreds of gentlemen who reside in the country, who keep large establishments of horses for the express purpose of hunting, and whose money might otherwise be spent in more questionable ways in town or elsewhere."

I have heard the following lines recited by one

who said that they ought to be put up over the mantelpiece of every farmer in the kingdom :—

>Attend, ye farmers, to this tale,
>And when ye mend the broken rail,
>Reflect with pleasure on a sport
>That lures your landlord from the court,
>To dwell and spend his rents among
>The country folk from whom they sprung;
>And should his steed with trampling feet
>Be urged across your tender wheat,
>*That steed*, perchance, *by you* was bred,
>And *yours the corn* by which he's fed,
>Ah! then restrain your rising ire,
>Nor rashly curse the hunting squire.—WARBURTON.

"So, Devonian, tell us thy history, for methinks 'twill be something strange."

DEVONIAN'S STORY

MY story must needs be a short one. In my own country I am called "The Bold Dragoon," and as every name either has or ought to have a particular meaning, I am so called in consequence of having once been in the possession of a certain captain of dragoons who lived in the far West. These are my facts. I was born and bred in a wild part of Devonshire, and when a year old fell into the possession of a keeper. To state exactly how such a thing happened might sometimes be inconvenient, as in hunting countries a man scarcely dares to confess the crime of capturing a fox, for lucre at least. But here the keeper, thinking me remarkable for size and strength, carried me to Captain T——,[1] who sent me off immediately as a present to Mr. G. Templar, the master of a pack of small foxhounds at Stover in Devonshire, and I was carried into a dark and gloomy place, which had been at first intended for a large stable, and was above seventy feet in length, and nearly the same in breadth. Here I was let loose, and looking about me in my fright, what should I see but at least twenty other foxes, all coiled up in the snug holes which they had made for themselves. Besides these there were others out of sight. They all took much care to hide themselves when any man came in. As soon as he who had brought me there had left the place, they all came round me. I soon learnt for what purpose I was brought hither, for it appeared that each of them had been separately hunted by this gentleman's hounds, which he had brought under such command, that they scarcely ever killed the fox they hunted; for when hunting up to him, if a rider was near enough to make his voice heard, and he rated or spoke to them, they would only bay at him till he was again captured, placed in a bag, and carried home again.

It rarely happened that not the master nor

[1] Captain Trelawney.—ED.

huntsman, nor the reverend friend who called himself first whipper-in, were up at the time, as they were generally mounted on thorough-bred horses, which they well knew how to ride. For myself, it is a well-known fact that I have been turned out and hunted by these hounds eighteen times, though I have striven hard to get away. On no occasion was I injured by the hounds, and I must do my possessor justice by stating that he thoroughly understands the nature of all the animals that he had to manage.

The extraordinary distance which we ran, when hunted by these hounds, may be attributed to our perfect ignorance of the country where we were turned out, which also accounts for our not oftener running at once to the impracticable parts which abound here, and in which no horses could have followed the hounds. In consequence of our knowing none of the coverts, we often ran straight across Dartmoor, where the scent was so good that the pace at which we were followed by the hounds made it often most severe work for us; and it became almost a relief to be taken up and replaced in the bag, which was carried for that purpose, and reconveyed to our gloomy prison, where we were well supplied with rabbits and other food.

The various habits of our race were most apparent. Some would keep quiet in their kennels, which were holes made by them in the ground, or where loose stones had been removed from the bottom of the wall which surrounded our prison, watching what was going on; whilst others were constantly moving about, as if in search of some outlet for escape. One, whose activity was extraordinary, had chosen for his place of rest a hole in the wall, being the opening intended for a window, which had been stopped up on the outside. It was full eight feet from the ground, and it was surprising, even to us, to see him run, with the greatest ease, up the perpendicular wall, as he daily did, aided by the roughness of the surface alone.

It now remains for me to explain how I am here and at liberty. We were one day surprised by the entrance of our feeder, who brought in several hampers, in which we were all taken to be turned out in the adjoining woods, there to shift for ourselves.

So you see that although I cannot boast of having beaten a pack of hounds, according to the tenor of the invitation, I have run away from them altogether, and am here to do you service by proving the error of the arch enemy, in thinking it absolutely necessary for his hounds to devour the animal they have been hunting, that their ardour in the chase may be increased. I have been sorely hunted by them, my friends, and not until they had won the day, and run up to their object, did they relax—not till then were they satisfied.

Again I would ask, why should our enemy wish to slaughter us when seeking refuge in an earth, up to which his hounds have hunted? seeing that those hounds so plainly show their contentment with having succeeded, and done all that was required of them.

All. "Bravo! bravo! well said, thou bold Dragoon!"

"Now, Berkshire, we pray thee tell us whether thou dost like a royal neighbourhood; whether thou art safer, and whether thy treatment there is preferable to our own. Tell us all that thou canst, as thou livest nearer to those parts than most of us do."

BERKSHIRE'S STORY

ON that score, my friends, I have not much to boast of; but having heard that the fair Queen had taken to herself a consort who rejoiced in the chase, I resolved to visit the royal forest. Soon I found that foxes here existed only in name. Some day in December I was lying in Windsor Forest about three o'clock in the afternoon, when I was disturbed by the voice of Sir J. Cope's huntsman, Shirley, who was taking the hounds through the forest to find a fox. Though so late, he was most persevering, and appeared determined to learn whether or not within the purlieus of the forest there was a fox left alive by the keepers. Seeing this I lost no time; but when stealing away was viewed by some of the hunters. The hounds soon followed me, and though it was a bad scenting day, I narrowly escaped. I saw enough of them to convince me that they were not to be trifled with, and that a tolerable scent would tax all my powers to beat them.

It was some years ago that I was lying in a covert at Billingbeare, when I was startled by Shirley's voice. I soon got away from the covert, thinking that I was not seen, but I was mistaken. A view-halloo was given, and the hounds were soon on my scent. I went the best pace I could straight towards and through the large woods at Shottesbrook, and onwards in the direction of Maidenhead thicket, where I passed through the middle of a small village. As the hounds had not been seen or heard, no one was looking out, and consequently no one saw me, although I passed through a cottage garden; and it behoves me to state that I probably owed my safety to nothing more dignified than a pig-sty attached to that garden, and which neutralised the scent; for the hounds soon afterwards hunting so far, were unable to hunt farther. It was supposed by the huntsman that I had taken refuge in some of the buildings, and a search was made; when a sportsman who was present expressed his surprise to a gentleman well-known in the hunt that they did not first hold on the hounds beyond the village, and make that good first; they would then have seen whether I had gone on or not, and if not it would have been time to come back and try all those places. This hint was taken, but too late to gain by it, for the scent, which the hounds had got on again, was now so cold that they could hunt me but slowly, instead of going at the pace they had hitherto gone, and which must have been the death of me had it been continued but a short time longer. I went straight on for several miles, until I reached the Thames near Cookham. I did not like to cross it, and returned to Bisham Wood; by which time, owing to my stopping about in a part of the wood, the hounds had got very near to me, when it luckily grew nearly dark; and though I was seen by them at not more than five hundred yards' distance, they were stopped and taken home, and I narrowly escaped from one of the most dashing packs in the kingdom. It is to be hoped by us in this part that his Royal Highness Prince Albert will have his commands obeyed by the keepers in Windsor Forest, and that this pack of hounds will not be driven elsewhere to find a fox. I now remained for a short time in a very thick covert, called Pigeon-House Coppice, through which I passed when hunted by the hounds.

There is a tragical story connected with this covert. The hounds many years since had met, and the gentlemen were all assembled, when the keeper who had the care of the coverts made his appearance, and producing a sack in which there was a fox, told them that unless they gave him a certain sum of money for it to turn out and hunt, he would shoot him before their eyes. This atrocious threat made them all quite furious, and they refused to give him anything; on which this monster in the shape of man immediately laid the sack which contained the fox on the ground, and according to his threat shot him dead. The rage which was felt by all present it is impossible to describe. They did not put him in his own sack and throw him into a pond close by; but he was soundly horsewhipped and instantly discharged from his place.

A much better feeling towards us now exists in this part of the country, and I have no longer a dread of being shot. But it is my intention to return to my old country, near Billingbeare and Shottesbrook, as I hear that the keepers there receive strict orders never to destroy one of us. This is the more handsome on the part of the occupier of the latter place, as he is not a fox-hunter himself. No doubt I shall be suffered to lie in the coverts of the former, though I find much of my food at Shottesbrook, where the coverts are so thin and hollow that I could not remain there during the day without many chances of being disturbed by the keeper's dogs. I hope at some future time to be able to tell you that the breed of foxes in those parts, and in the royal purlieus, has so increased that it has been unnecessary for me to risk my life very often with Sir J. Cope's fine pack of hounds. It is reported that he intends to pay more frequent visits to these parts in future, in consequence of having given up the distant part of the country.

"And now, Sandy, tell us what is going on north of Tweed. Be there any hounds there? It is reported that foxes there are shot like rabbits. The mountains, it seems, are not to be rode over, and so no fox-hunting; is it so?"

SANDY'S STORY

LET me at once undeceive you upon one point. It is not the mountains there, but the hounds, that are hard to be rode over, and that on account of the scent. We have, however, noble lords and others who can and do keep with the hounds, except on the steepest parts of the Cheviots. In the next place, let me pray of you not to believe the slanderers who say that we are so unmercifully slaughtered. No, my friends, it is not so. We have patrons as good as, if not better, than you have in the South. One gentleman alone has lately raised, at his own expense, for our sole use, a series of coverts, which was the only thing required, as both sides of Tweed, Berwickshire, and Northumberland are as fine country as can be desired, and, unfortunately for us, as good scenting as any in the kingdom.

It is supposed that when people can fly thither by steam, it will become the Melton of the North; but I hope the idea will end, as it began, in smoke. You, my southern friends, appear to think that we do not go the very fast pace that you do, and that the hounds by which we are hunted are not equally as good as those in your country; but in this, too, you are much mistaken. So good is the scent there that, if it were not for the drains, which are now so general in the cultivated parts, the hounds, at the awful pace they go, would in a very short time kill nearly every one of us. Then the huntsmen are not to be despised; on the contrary, we have to contend with one who, with the following qualifications, is near perfection,—the eye of an eagle, fine temper, boldness, enterprise, coolness, perseverance, intelligence, and, above all, decision. This is the rare man with whom, and with whose pack, we have to contend. I am proud to say that I have been hunted by, and escaped from him, on a good scenting day too, by taking refuge in the crevice of a rock, after one of the fastest runs possible for five miles. It began thus:—One morning early last season, when lying in a covert called Bushen Glen, I was startled by hearing a man riding quickly by. He then suddenly stopped and addressed these few words to the whipper-in, who brought the hounds.

"How long have you been here?"

"Just come, my lord."

"Is Mr. Smith here?"

"Not yet, my lord."

"Well, I never was so thoroughly drenched; never rode twenty-four miles in such a deluge; so, by Jove, I can't wait. Give me my horse."

No sooner done, than "Cover hoick!" reached my astonished ears, and I instantly left my kennel prepared for a start. In a few minutes I was stealing away, and after clearing the wall and running in the open moor, I passed near the gentleman, I suppose, who was expected, and who, on seeing me, said not a word. I therefore, thinking I was unseen, did not turn back to the covert, but, laying my ears well back on my poll, took straight away across the moor, and just had a glimpse of the hounds and their noble huntsman, Lord Elcho,[1] topping the wall at the same time. My flight,

---

[1] Father of the present Earl of Wemyss. He continued to hunt this country till about 1868.

"Topping the Wall."

however, was too rapid to allow time for much curiosity. This was enough to make me go my best pace straight across the moor for four miles, and then a mile or two beyond, over fields, till I reached a hanging covert on a steep by the side of the Whitadder River, at which time the hounds were not more than four hundred yards from me. Although they did not see me, they ran the whole way as if they really did.

Here, although there was soon another fox or two moving, they still went on with my scent; for with the most unerring judgment this huntsman kept the pack from changing, till at length I crossed the river and over the moor on the other side to a place of refuge, a crevice in a rock, for I could not go farther. The gentlemen rode up, and I heard these words: "Well, I never saw a finer run. During the first four miles the tail hounds never got to the head at all, though not one hundred yards behind those that were leading when they first started."

On other occasions I have saved my life in a similar way, but a circumstance occurred which almost made me resolve never again to resort to a drain. I was one night crossing a farm, not many miles from Dunse, when I heard cries as of a fox in distress, and on going to the spot whence the noise proceeded I discovered that two of my brethren were confined in a stone drain, where they had been several days without food, and were nearly starved. I used every exertion in my power to scratch away the stones which had been placed to stop up the entrance, in order to prevent a fox going into it, as Lord Elcho's hounds were to meet near it next day. Fortunately Mr. Wilson, the owner of the land, passed that way and saw that the ground and stones had been lately disturbed by me, when he removed them, and saw the two foxes, one of which was found dead shortly after. He ascertained that his man had stopped them in nine days before, and that he forgot to open the drain again.

I once crossed the Tweed at a dangerous part, thinking that I should, by so doing, leave the hounds and all behind. Not so; for the huntsman was not to be stopped, but swam his horse, as two or three others did, across the river, Treadwell, Mr. Robertson's[1] huntsman, taking the lead. Having thus crossed the river without gaining my point, and running in a ring of several miles, I recrossed the river at a spot where it was impossible for

[1] The late Mr. Robertson of Ladykirk.—ED.

horses to cross; so that, being a long way round, the hounds were stopped, and it was agreed that I was drowned in the Tweed.

Having seen some part of the country on the English side of the Tweed, I determined to cross back to it; and after being there a short time only, and lying in a field of large turnips, not uncommon in this part, I was awakened by hearing a loud voice: "Treadwell, I wish you would draw the hounds through this turnip field. It is a very likely place to find a fox." This order was obeyed with the utmost silence; but fortunately, having had the previous notice, I was off and away as fast as my legs could carry me, and was not seen, owing to the height of the turnips, until I reached the next field. The hounds soon got on my scent, and pursued me closely for about twenty-five minutes, so extremely fast, that I began to think I had changed my country for the worse.

Independently of their great speed, I could not hear them, as I did those by which I had been hunted on the other side of Tweed. I reached in safety a small covert, in passing through which it appeared that the hounds got on the scent of another fox, which turned out to be a cub, and so I escaped; for although an old sportsman saw me after I left the covert going apparently much distressed, and evidently the hunted fox, yet the hounds were not allowed to be taken from that which they were running, which it appeared they some time afterwards killed, scarcely having left the covert.

I had one or two more escapes from this determined huntsman and his killing pack, which escapes I attributed to my good luck in having been hunted by them on bad scenting days, and also in taking refuge in drains. Learning that many of my friends had been killed by them, I was induced to move into Roxburghshire, the country hunted by the Duke of Buccleuch's hounds, and adjoining the two hunts before described to you. There I had not been long before I was found in a small covert by the Duke's pack, as Williamson the huntsman[1] calls it, though he seems to do just what he likes with it. Be that as it may, he knew pretty well where to find me, and it was done in a few minutes. The hills form a part of the country that he surpasses most men in riding across; and after running over them for some time towards the Cheviots, the blue tops of which seemed at the time to be higher

[1] Williamson was pensioned off in 1865 and died a year or two later. Shore, who succeeded him, still carries the horn.—ED.

than the clouds, the hounds came to a check, owing as it was thought, to my having overtaken some cattle, and to too much delay in holding on the hounds; and I escaped.

It appeared to me that these hounds had at the time rather too much flesh, though shortly afterwards the fault was mended; for I never was pressed more by any pack in my life. Every hound seemed to go as if he had the leading scent. All came nearly abreast for several fields, and they were close to me when I again took refuge in a drain. The extraordinary scent just described induces me to relate the events of that day from the beginning. A remark was made before the hounds had thrown off, by an old sportsman, as follows. It happened that several coverts were drawn by the hounds without their finding a fox, although it was notorious that foxes had been on every former day most abundant there; on hearing this the gentleman said, "I have often observed that on good scenting days foxes are not to be found, even where they are known to abound as they do here."

"How do you account for that?" was asked.

"Probably on these good scenting days foxes lie under ground, or in places not disturbed by hounds, for as they live by the use of their noses, they cannot but know their danger of being hunted on such days."

The hounds were taken on some distance towards another covert, but on passing by a small piece of gorse, not half an acre across, they were taken quietly to it, and in a short time killed a fox which had not moved from his kennel. This created some amusement at the expense of the gentleman who had stated his belief that it was a good scenting day, and some one said—

"Now, what do you think?"

"Why, that I am now more sure of it: for if this fox had moved under the circumstances when the hounds were so close to him, the scent being a good one, would have made it almost certain death: and so his best chance of escape was to lie still: but he has been too cunning."

Rather more than the hallooing usual when a dead fox is given to hounds took place; and the three men appeared to be trying who could oftenest repeat, "Tally-ho!" The hounds were again taken on towards the next large covert, and no sooner were they in it than they all threw their tongues and ran as if close to a fox, which was not the case, for it happened to be my own scent, and I having heard the dreadful hallooing before described, and knowing it to be a good scenting day, had moved away some time before the hounds had reached the covert, although the crash they made there seemed as if close to me. I then ran as described before, straight to a drain about three or four miles off; but although I had so good a start they nearly overtook me before I reached it. Waiting near the entrance I overheard the following remarks:—

"How very unlucky, just as the hounds were running into him. Such a swift pace they came, he could not have stood it five minutes longer." I then distinctly heard the gentleman alluded to before exclaim, "Well! I shall not be surprised if there are half a dozen foxes in this drain; somewhere they must be."

Then another voice, "Well, Will, what do you think now of Mr. Smith's foresay as to its being a good scenting day?"

"My lord, he was right; I never in all my life saw the hounds run so fast—faster they could not go." He suddenly turned towards the man who ought to have stopped the drain. "Hoot, mon, how is this? The earth's open at yer vary ain door!"

"Will, where's the terrier?"

"Got none, my lord."

"Was ever the like? Seventeen years I have hunted with these hounds, and though every field in this country is full of drains, they have never had a terrier that was worth hanging. Jack, go and fetch the farmer's terrier; be off like a shot! How can they expect to save their poultry if they do not put gratings to their drains? Without them it is impossible for hounds to kill their foxes."

Having by this time recovered my breath, I began to move away from the entrance, when to my surprise I found that there were no less than three foxes in the drain beside myself. Having with great difficulty forced myself past the first I came against, and whilst waiting anxiously the result, we were all much frightened by suddenly seeing a glimpse of light some distance up the drain beyond us. The men had dug a hole through the top of the drain at that spot; and shortly after this we heard them trying to force a rough terrier of the real Makerston breed to enter; they at length succeeded, when he immediately came down straight towards us. Not a little alarmed, and each of us struggling and striving to get away first, out we

T. Smith, Esq., del. "EVERY HOUND HAS GOT A FOX!" CRIED OLD WILL. *Facing page 121.*

all bolted, with the terrier close at our heels. The scene which followed it is almost impossible to describe. The first fox was pursued by the greatest number of hounds, and, as I came second, the next greatest number followed me; and so after us they came; but our sally was so sudden that we fortunately had gained the start of them by some ten or twenty yards.

I think I still hear the voice of old Will crying out, "Every hound has got a fox!" As I jumped over the fence, he was still holding his whip in the air, undecided which of the four lots (into which the hounds had divided) he should follow. So good was the scent on that day, that although only about four couples of hounds followed me, I went straight to another drain; and, strange to say, there found another of the same party as before, which accounted for the two first lots of hounds leaving a short time before they ran up to the earth. Here our lives were again in danger; and, hearing the men again digging at some distance, I profited by what had passed, and pushed beyond it. My unfortunate fellow was again forced out by the same terrier, and fell a victim to our foes; who, not suspecting that another fox was in the earth, again left me.

"Well, Will, do you recollect the foresay about there being half a dozen foxes in the last drain?"

"I do, my lord; and now the gentleman's foresays have all been fulfilled from beginning to end."

During the time they were waiting for the terrier at the last drain, and doubting whether he could be found, a farmer was filling in the stones at the entrance of the drain, and being asked what he was about, he answered,—"Why, if the terrier don't come, we will starve the fox to death, which is easy to do in this drain. He has had mony fowls; about forty I ken."

"What's that?" said the Southron. "Pretty sort of encouragement for a gentleman to spend so much money in the country in keeping hounds. Why, the Duke pays more money to the farmers in one week than all the poultry in the hunt would sell for in a twelvemonth; to say nothing of all that is spent in it by the gentlemen who hunt. If there were no foxes there would be no hounds."

"Vary true, vary true," was the reply; "but Mr. Williamson is raather too closefisted when he pays a bittie o' the Duke's siller."

The worst part of the story, as relates to ourselves, remains to be told, namely, that when they left a hard bargain was going on for the purchase of the terrier which had driven us out of our retreat, and he was to be taken to the kennel for the same employment when required, which, sure enough, was often the case. Luckily for me he was not with the hounds a short time after, when I was again found by this pack, as I lay in a wood near Floors, belonging to the Duke of Roxburgh, who, though no fox-hunter, is one of our best friends, and gives his keepers strict orders never to destroy us. But for the absence of this terrier I must have been in jeopardy that day; for having heard the hounds running after another fox, I was just stepping away to a drain close to the Tweed, in a contrary direction, not before I was seen, and a few hounds got on my scent, which they followed until they reached the drain where I was. On being told of which, old Will, the huntsman, brought the rest of the hounds to the spot, determined to get me out. Tools were procured, and several attempts were made, but in vain. Some half-bred terriers were then sent for, but they would not venture near me, nor could they a second time be urged to go in. Other fruitless attempts were made, and a great part of the morning was lost in this way by a throng of hunters, and amongst them the noble master of the pack. Whilst this was going on, and they were looking at and admiring the beauties of the stately river, a large salmon leaped clean out of the water, as if on purpose to amuse or to tantalise them. Whereupon a gentleman present asked his Grace if it would give him pleasure to have a throw with a fly for such a fish. His fit reply might well be a source of satisfaction and pleasure to all who hunt in countries where his Grace has property.

"To tell the truth I care little for that kind of sport; but, as to the other, I am never perfectly happy unless I have on a red coat."

All at length left the place exceedingly annoyed that the terrier, the hero of the former day, had not been with them. Probably the bargain for him was not completed, and consequently I escaped.

Wishing to return to my old haunts, I had got as far as a covert called the Hirsel, belonging to Lord Home, where I had not been long when one day I heard two reports, which turned out to be from the keeper's gun, discharged at two innocent young fox-hound puppies, thus deliberately butchered for having strayed by chance from the hospitable home of the kind mistress whose pets they were, and whose gentle care and caresses they had so often enjoyed. You will not be surprised when I tell you that our race appears to be almost extinct about these woods.

After this tragical event I lost no time, but went to the farthest covert belonging to this estate, and nearly surrounded by Lord Elcho's country. I hoped to be there as far as possible from danger, and thought myself secure, as the outside covert was kept quiet, and scarcely disturbed even by the hounds of the Duke in whose hunt it is retained. It is suspected that the keeper kills all of us foxes that he can in that part, because no hounds hunt it enough. He says that all the foxes in Lord Elcho's country come there to be quiet. Be that as it may, the last time the hounds found me there they had before drawn all the other woods, and only found one fox, and that a mangy one. I was disturbed first by hearing old Will cheering his hounds, as if he had just seen a fox, giving his cheer thus, "Hooi-here, here, here!" which, in any other country, would pass for a view-halloo.

After listening and expecting to hear the hounds in full cry, I found it was only his customary cry in drawing a whin covert, particularly when he wished his hounds to get into it. I noticed that they did not attend to the halloo so readily when a fox was really seen. Notwithstanding this, they understood their huntsman's system well enough to make it no safe thing to be hunted by them. I soon left the covert, and when they had pursued me for some miles, and were getting nearer to me, they suddenly came to a check; on looking back, I saw the huntsman almost immediately take them away beyond the next large field, rather to the left of where my line was hitherto pointing; I suppose either because there was a flock of sheep in that field, or because he thought I had gone to a covert in that direction. If the hounds had had their time, they would have hit off the scent to the right of the field. The upshot was, that I, thinking that they had given me up, took the first opportunity of getting out of sight, not because I was tired and beaten, as some suppose must always be the case when we seek such places of refuge; which they soon ascertained was the case, for nearly as soon as the hounds had hunted up to the drain on one side of the road, I started off on the other, and though they had as good a start with me as they could wish for, I contrived to run away from them, owing to the scent not being good enough for hounds to kill a stout fox without assistance; and probably to the huntsman repeating his former mistake in making an injudicious forward cast when not wanted. He did not now venture to hold the hounds forward and across the line I came, or else they would have got on the scent, as I returned nearly the same way, which was ascertained by a hunter on his return home, a man having seen me.

Having escaped from this lively pack of hounds, I did not venture to remain in this part, but at once took up my abode near Foulden, where I was again found by Lord Elcho and his pack, though I fancied I had selected an out-of-the-way spot near the river Whitadder, with which part I was well acquainted, as his lordship has reason to know and to regret. After they had hunted me some time, finding myself distressed, I was induced to return to my old haunts, creeping along a narrow track by the side of the steep and rocky bank which overhung the river, the height of which, where I passed, was nearly a hundred feet. Several of these high-couraged hounds in attempting to follow me lost their footing, fell to the bottom, and were killed. It was only strange that a single hound escaped; and though I certainly did not intend to assist in preventing their destruction, yet such happened to be the case; for having waited, when in my narrow track, for some time, and thinking myself safe, I heard the piercing cry of a hound, which I then believed was following me. I ran straight along the top of the precipice, and was seen by the whipper-in and some of the hounds, and the noise they instantly made by hallooing a view with all their might, assisted by his lordship blowing his horn, attracted the notice of the other hounds, or they would otherwise have followed on the line to certain destruction. I attribute my escape to the powerful effect this event had on the feelings of the owner of the pack. Lest I should again lead them back to the same spot, he immediately took them off my scent and sent them home, and I flattered myself that we should never again see these hounds run to find a fox in this part of the country; for the anguish created in his lordship's mind it is impossible for me to describe, although it may be easily imagined.

However, all my hopes of living a quiet life here were destroyed. A great friend of his lordship's, and of ours, Mr. Wilkie of Foulden, near where this occurred, and on whose rabbits I sometimes subsisted, immediately took measures to prevent the same calamity from happening again; and although it was hitherto pronounced an impossibility, he has, as far as I at present can judge of it, succeeded. It was managed by cutting away my narrow track at the edge of the rock which overhung the river. To do this required much labour and risk; but it was effected by suspending a ladder, which was fastened by strong ropes to stakes driven in the ground some distance above. I need not say that I watched the work with no great satisfaction; and as I saw the foundation of my once favourite track fall into the river below, when they gradually broke it away, it made my heart ache. I felt that I must now either stay and be killed, or move into another country. I decided on the latter.

Although I vowed in an hour of distress, when first hunted by the hounds there, never to run the risk of them again if I escaped, I recrossed the Tweed into England, and have taken up my quarters on one of the highest parts of the Cheviot Hills, hoping to find a safe retreat from them. There are, however, dangers to be dreaded there, as well as in every country where hounds are not kept to hunt us; but the system of destruction to be dreaded by me is one that is adopted on mountainous parts alone. The shepherds of the mountains on certain days gather together against us, armed with guns, and aided by dogs of all sorts, from the greyhound to the collie. The sagacity and docility of the latter are very astonishing; but the sagacity of an old dog of the fox-hound sort is superior to that of every other. The collie dog is taught by man what to do, whilst the old fox-hound teaches his master. Had it not been for the sagacity of the hound, I should have been spared many a perilous run. The shepherds pretend that the breed of the mountain fox is of a different kind from our own, and that the head of the male is larger. For my own part, I believe the animals to be of the same kind as ourselves, and to be merely larger altogether; for I have sometimes met one in my rambles. Their superior size may be accounted for as follows: having been born or bred in the wholesome air upon the mountains, where food, such as rabbits, is probably scarce, they find and fatten upon sheep which from various accidents die there. Having once got a taste for such food, it is not surprising that they will take a lamb, or attack an old one which has fallen through illness or neglect. Anxious as I am to protect my own race, I cannot blame the shepherds for waging war against the transgressors; as it is known that when once a fox has taken to such a habit, he seldom gives it up but with his life. Felons are to be found everywhere; but, as to ourselves, the following facts will prove that the generality of us are not guilty of charges frequently laid upon us. On the first day of February last, being the last day of pheasant shooting, I was lying in a thick plantation, in the middle of a park at Ladykirk, on the other side of the Tweed, which covered a space of ground not more than a quarter of an acre, when a party were shooting not far off, and I suddenly heard one of them exclaim, "Look out, there goes a fox! he jumped up close by me. There he goes, straight away. I wish the hounds were here."

In the course of an hour after this, I was again startled by hearing, "Tally-ho! tally-ho! there goes another fox! Don't mistake him for a hare, and shoot him; he's close to you, in the clump between!" And then again the same loud voice,— "There he goes, right across the park; what a fine fellow he is!"

It shortly afterwards became my turn to exhibit. They came to the clump where I was, and a man who went in beyond directly called out, "There goes a hen pheasant, there go two, three!" and so on. He had just cried out, "That makes thirteen hen pheasants!" when a spaniel rushed into the thick bushes, and obliged me to face the whole party. A glorious cheering they gave me; and when they had expressed their surprise and satisfaction, the keeper assured them of his belief, that there were as many pheasants left as had been there at the beginning of the season, excepting those that had been shot by sportsmen. Now if I, or any of us, were so much given to destroy game as we are reported to be, there would not have been a pheasant left alive in a week's time from the beginning of the season, whereas it was now nearly the end of it. This fortunately occurred in the presence of several persons, who saw all three of us. No less than five other foxes from the same park have been killed by Lord Elcho and his pack this season.

Hoping that I have given you all sufficient encouragement to induce you to make us a visit in the north, I conclude my story.

CONCLUSION

ONE more friend was about to begin his story. Whether he was from York, Lincoln, Nottingham, or Bedfordshire, was not ascertained, for on a sudden we were startled by the cawing of an old crow and the screams of a jay, which, added to the chatterings of a couple of magpies, warned us that daylight was appearing; and I was reluctantly obliged to request that his story might be deferred to some future time, should we ever meet again, when we might all have more to relate concerning the inexhaustible subject of our lives. Chanticleer now clapped admiring wings, and sang out a loud applause. This excited the particular notice of one of our party, who exclaimed, "I'll go round and have a sly bite at his tail, for 'tis a quiet retired place, and no one yet about."

"Take heed," said I, "that thou bring us not into trouble."

Soon afterwards we were again interrupted by

the clamour of those tell-tale birds; for it seems that our friend was returning without his intended booty, having been seen by the keeper, who fast approached towards us. Therefore, hastily bidding adieu until we should meet again, we all returned to our favourite coverts.

EXTRACTS

FROM THE

DIARY OF A HUNTSMAN

PREFACE

THE writer, a master of fox-hounds for some years, is aware that it will be easy to discover that these observations were not designed to appear in the world, written as they were for his own satisfaction alone, until the repeated requests of many induced him to offer them; possibly owing to the circumstances of having hunted his own hounds with fair success, and the fact of having killed ninety foxes in ninety-one days' hunting, one season, in a bad scenting country. If they should be read and chance to amuse, well and good; reputation by writing them was not the object sought. They were put down just as they came into his head, principally on his return in the evening after hunting. Therefore he does not affect so strict an observance of rules as one who makes a profession of writing, and gains a reputation by his pen, else they should have been arranged in a better method. Although acquired by study, long thought, and strict observation, if they have any value, it is their originality. His hope is, by attempting to make them sharp, short, and decisive, to induce men to read them; and if they should be the means of promoting the taste for *hunting*—a sport to which this country is indebted for the superiority of its officers over most other nations, etc., as well as the social feeling which it creates in the country where hounds are kept—he will have gained his point.

CHAPTER I

HUNTSMAN

. . . by chase our forefathers earn'd their food,
Toil strung their nerves and purified their blood.

N early find is desirable, and, as the huntsman should always be at the head, it is right to commence these observations with him; for on him not only does the sport in general depend, but the cheer of a good one when he first finds his fox, creates that indescribable sensation which nothing else has ever been known to do. Who can hear the cheer of the huntsman, added to the cry of the hounds and the blowing of the horn, without being inspired? Indeed it is quite a source of regret whenever a clever huntsman has not naturally a pleasant, melodious voice, instead of one probably that may be compared to the grunting of a pig—which has been the case before now. When this is the case, he should try every method to improve it. It should be recollected, that many men who go out with hounds have no opportunity of enjoying the sport beyond the find, which is, with the assistance of the voice, often one of the best parts of the day's sport; but to make it so *vox et præterea nihil* will not do, for unless he has a soul for sport, even when most in earnest he cannot cause such delightful sensations to thrill through you as ought, and as always did, by the voice of such a man as old Luke, huntsman to the late Duke of Richmond, and Lord Egremont.

To be perfect, a huntsman should possess the following qualifications: health, memory, decision, temper, and patience, a good ear, voice, and sight, courage and spirits, perseverance and activity; and with these he will soon make a bad pack a good one: if quick, he will make a slow pack quick; if slow, he will make a quick pack slow. But first, to become a good one, he must have a fair chance, and should not be interfered with by any one after he leaves the place of meeting; previous to which, on all occasions, it would be best if the master of the hounds was to arrange with him which covers should be drawn first, etc. It rarely happens that two men think exactly alike, and unless he is capable of judging for himself after the above arrangement (which had much better be made overnight), the master is to blame in keeping him; but if he is capable, the master is to blame for interfering; for, consequently, the man will be ever thinking—what does master think? and will not gain that independence of thought and action so necessary on most occasions to be a match for a fox. For instance, at a check there are many, apparently trifling ideas and thoughts in a huntsman's head which he cannot explain to his master, when asked why he does this or that. Instead of answering, he drops his bridal-hand and listens to his master, although he has made observation of trifles, which are often all he has for his guidance and frequently are sufficient to recover his fox, though probably no other person noticed them,—such as this: the pack is running best pace; he sees one hound turn his head and fling to the right or left a pace or two; shortly after there is a check (say 500 yards). When he has made the usual casts, he recollects the hound turning his head, and then goes back and finds that the fox had headed back so far, and hits off the scent; but he could or would not tell any one why he was going back. It is such like trifling observations that huntsmen profit by, though unnoticed by others. It is true, many men who keep hounds are good sportsmen; but then, unless the huntsman is a fool, he soon finds it out, and gladly looks for a hint from his master when at a loss; in short, he must be allowed and encouraged to have a good opinion of himself, or he will not gain confidence; and if he has not that, he will not have the first and greatest qualification, namely, decision. A want of this has saved half the foxes now living in hunting countries. It is not here meant, that for want of decision huntsmen do nothing; they go on, it is true, but in their own minds have not decided on what sort of cast to make, or what to be at; therefore, the huntsman should never be taken by surprise, but be constantly on the lookout for mischief, he will thus gain decision.

It is necessary for a huntsman to be thoroughly acquainted with the nature of the animal he is hunting, and also that he hunts with; for he will learn more from them than from the whole world besides. From the fox he will learn cunning; and from an old hound, sagacity. In short, he will do well when in chase to consider what he would do was *he* himself the fox he is hunting; thereby he will always anticipate a check, and cast his hounds the way he should have gone had he been the fox,— which, it may generally be observed, will be a line of country where he would avoid being seen, unless there is some local cause for it. By attending to this, he will be prepared for a check in many instances a mile before he gets to it, if he knows the country, and keeps his eyes open; he must, to do this, have only half an eye for the pack, and the other eye and half beyond it; and he will also soon discover whether the fox is one he has hunted before by the line he takes, and other peculiarities, —even the ring he takes in cover, the rack he uses in fences,—which observations are of great assistance a second time, but more particularly so later in the season, for a whole litter of young foxes have been known to run the same line of country.

Other observations in chase are worthy of notice. He will find it no uncommon thing for a fox in chase to pass over several earths which are not stopped, and go on straight for several miles beyond them; but when he finds that he cannot shake off the pack, and is a little distressed, he will head back to the nearest earth he has come over which was open, and go to ground, unless the whipper-in is desired to clap back quickly and get there first and stop it, or stand on it, if, as in a neighbouring country, the laws of fox-hunting do not allow a whipper-in to stop it. But it is no uncommon thing when a fox heads back in this way to an earth, if the whipper-in gets there first, for the fox to be killed immediately on the earth, so very nearly do they calculate their remaining strength. This knowledge and recollection of the fox having passed over earths which are supposed to be open, will be a guide for a huntsman to make a cast, if beaten out of scent, by cold hunting back.

In the first place, it will be necessary to find your fox, which you will best do by drawing up wind, or he will find you, and be off, if a good one, before you are aware of it; and this, was there no other, would be a sufficient reason. Hounds naturally draw up wind to any scent or drag of a fox, and early in the season it is of the greatest consequence to young hounds, if, when some are running riot, most likely *down* wind, behind the huntsman, they can hear his voice, and then a rate and a smack of the whip from the whipper-in sends them on to him at once; but if the huntsman was down wind of *them*, though they may stop at the rate, not hearing him go at it again, they would probably be left to run riot for the day. Even if the pack have found and went away they would not hear it, being up wind; but, if they were left down wind and the pack were running, then the young hounds must hear it, and would most probably join the cry.

Different men have different ways of drawing covers, but there can be no doubt that the best way to make a pack draw well is, to go steadily through covers with hounds, where it is possible; if not, then to take the best side-wind of it first. When a cover is supposed to be drawn, a huntsman will do well to notice whether he has got all his hounds. If any old ones are left back, he may depend on it there is some good cause—no doubt a stroke of a fox or drag keeps them—and a little patience, and even encouragement by name, may be thought right, particularly if they happen to be hounds that usually find, and in all packs there are a few of that sort.

There is another method of drawing, which cannot be thought a good one by sportsmen in general, though it is not unusual. The huntsman throws his hounds into a cover, through which he cannot ride, and is obliged to keep outside. As soon as the hounds are in, away he trots round the outside, thinking that by getting to the opposite side of the cover he will be able to draw them through by his voice; but the consequence is that three parts of the pack, hearing him trot away, turn their heads and follow outside, and are apt to be on the watch for it ever afterwards. Had he gone steadily on, though outside, they would have drawn it properly. That hounds should be apt to dread being left behind is not much to be wondered at, considering the quickness with which they get away after their fox.

When hounds are not in the habit of drawing furze (in the upper countries called gorse or whins), they will draw it best in the morning, when there is a drag into it; and by going round the cover quietly they will feel it, and go well in. By going on round it, the hounds will also find all the open parts and more readily get in, than if the huntsman rides up to one side only, and then tries to force them to go in; than which nothing has a more disgusting effect.

In large covers it often happens that several foxes are on foot at the same time, and there is great difference of opinion whether, if your hounds are running a fox, or more than one, and another is viewed away from the cover, you should get your hounds off the fox they are running and take the flyer; or stick to the one they are running. If sport is the object, decidedly the flyer is the fox to give it. Another reason for adopting this plan is that, after the season begins, the field have a right to expect sport. But if it is necessary to rattle covers, and stay in them for the purpose of making all the foxes fly, it should be done before regular hunting begins, or have a by-day for it now and then; otherwise, a whole season may pass without a run from this cover, for there are foxes that never will break cover. Of course, if no fox goes away, these must be killed if you can. But such covers as these generally do hold a stranger that has probably been hunted so much in his native covers that he is on a quiet visit only, and goes home at the first notice when he hears the huntsman's voice. After the first of February it should be a rule to get away with the first fox, as you may otherwise get on a vixen; indeed most of the good runs are from large covers, and generally with a dog fox.

The writer not long since met the pack belonging to a noble Duke when they were drawing a large cover. His Grace politely expressed his regret that it was a bad cover to get away from with hounds; the reply was that generally the best runs are from such covers, as the fox can get away without being headed as they are in small covers, when every tailor out wishes to get a view of him. During this conversation a fox broke away from the other side, and they got well settled to him and after a good run killed, which is not often the case when found in this way; for the fox has time to prepare himself, and will hang about the cover until he is fit to go, during which he is abused as a dunghill brute, etc., but when he does go, catch him who can. But the same fox which has beaten hounds into fits almost, if he had been whipped up out of his kennel in a bit of gorse, would not have stood a burst of twenty minutes. A little observation in the upper countries may prove the above, for if a fox hangs about in a bit of gorse for half an hour or so before he breaks, it takes a great deal to kill him, though the pack were close at him when he started. And there are foxes that can beat any hounds, if they have time to prepare themselves, and have a fair start.

In most covers there is a favourite quarter which

holds a fox, and the sooner that is drawn the better; for if it is a good scenting day and there is a drag, the fox is aware of it, and will be off the moment he hears the huntsman's voice; therefore, as no man can tell till he has tried whether it is a good scenting day or not, he should adopt the safe plan and find him quickly if he can, particularly if late in the year. A fox generally lies where the rays of the sun can reach him during the day,—in two-year-old coppice wood, etc. It is worthy of notice that one cover will generally hold a fox, when another adjoining it seldom or ever does. By the middle of the season a huntsman will, or ought to, know where to put his hand on a fox (if there is one in the country), let him be in what part he may, but to do this he must be very observant on all occasions.

To have even spirits (not easily dejected) is also a requisite for a huntsman, otherwise on bad scenting seasons he will often go home without his fox, and will be apt to feel disheartened, and that he is never to kill another. But this will not do, although his hounds after a continuation of it will scarcely turn to a halloo, and it requires the patience of Job to put up with what one hears and sees; for some men will say, it is all the huntsman's fault that the hounds will not draw; some, it is the fault of the hounds; others, that they are too high fed; others, too low; in short, no end to complaints. But a change of scent does come; and the same hounds which would not leave his horse's heels, no sooner get sight of the cover they are to draw, than in they fly, and not a hound is to be seen, find their fox, and turn at a word across flints and fallows, and probably kill every fox they find for weeks following. This again requires evenness of spirits, else the delusive conceit that he can kill any fox with half a scent, will only be the cause of greater annoyance on a return to bad scent. It is not meant that he should feel indifferent whether he killed or not; for if he could go home, to bed, and to sleep, without satisfying himself as to what became of his fox, he would not do for *some* people.

It is no uncommon thing to hear men who have nothing to do with the hounds say, "Well, never mind; we have had a good day's sport. He is a good fox, and will show us another," etc. This is all very well, but it will not do for a huntsman. The better the run, the more anxious he will be to kill, or run to ground; for, without either, it is not perfect, and may be compared to a fox without a brush,—having the matchless beauties combined, and yet not perfect; for he should always give an account of his fox if he can. And if he wishes to have plenty, he must kill them; for, however strange it may appear, it is the only way to ensure a stock in the country; and at the same time you secure the support and assistance of the farmers, and those keepers who are not maliciously disposed, when it is known that you do kill all you can, and do not go home satisfied by saying, "Oh! we have had a good run, and he will show us another"; then they will not kill them. But how can it be supposed that any farmer will like the thought of seeing the same ground and fences ridden over constantly, owing to one particular fox being too stout to be killed by hounds, or that there is no wish to kill him? or can it be the same pleasure to be always riding the same line of country? Therefore it is right to kill when you can.

That a huntsman should be a bold rider is proved by every check the hounds come to when he is away; for even when he is present, he will have enough to do to prevent overriding. But, unless he can ride at the head and see the very spot on which they throw up, he will be puzzled to know whom to apply to of those forward, and must often use his own judgment; in short, the greatest use he can be of, when there is a good scent, is to prevent men doing mischief. Therefore he must have nerve to ride well up, and equal to any man in the kingdom; for, unless he can be forward enough to look men in the face, and request them to hold hard, he may ride behind and call after them till he is hoarse, and they will not turn their heads—probably believing that jealousy alone is the cause, and they go the faster for it; but if he is in his place, none but a madman will do mischief if requested to pull up; even the hard riders from the universities (that is, if they can stop their horses) will do so. But if a huntsman feels obliged to speak on these occasions, it should be *at* them rather than *to* them; thus—" Hold hard; pray, black horse, hold hard!" Few men like to be attacked by name, even when they have done mischief, nor does a huntsman feel comfortable if he has been led to speak sharply in the heat of the chase; for, on second thoughts, he will recollect that it was the ardour which he most likes to see, that led them on.

It is not only right that a huntsman should keep with his hounds in the open, but it is of the greatest consequence for him to do so when his hounds are running in cover; particularly if the fox has been hunted, and at all beaten. He must not allow

anything to make him lose the cry of the pack, but keep within hearing at all hazards; for, although it sometimes appears that all is going so well, that he may stand still and let them come round, and that he will meet them. But if he does this he will surely repent it, nine times out of ten; something is certain to happen, when least expected; the merest trifle may bring them to a check, which he would have seen and got over, had he been there; therefore, *never leave them*. If no other means, he should keep down wind enough; for if they divide when he does not hear the leading hounds, he is just as likely to go away with a fresh fox as not, and leave his beaten one in the cover, which is the cause of so many foxes escaping. But if he does stick to them, and never lose the cry of the leading hound, even if only one, when they divide, he gets on with the right, and, by cheering and the use of the horn, he may keep to his right fox. Although the crash with the other lot is much greater, this hound will not leave the hunted one; and if a whipper-in is active, he will soon stop the others, even if there be eighteen couple out of twenty running the fresh fox. When an old fox has come some distance, and is a little beaten, he turns so short in cover, that, unless a huntsman is within hearing when he does come up at a check, he is at a loss how to act, and had better stand perfectly quiet, and let the old hounds do it, or it is probable he will do mischief by holding them either way; besides, it does hounds so much harm not letting them get out of difficulties themselves—in cover particularly. But had he been up at the check, or near enough to have heard which way the leading hound was bearing, he might have profited by it, if they did not hit it off quickly. Here it is where foxes beat hounds, principally owing to a huntsman not exerting himself to the very utmost; but, fancying that the hounds will be sure to kill him, they foolishly think it of no consequence, and take it too quietly.

More foxes are lost when dead beaten than at any other time; and here show their superior cunning, by the wonderful tricks they play the hounds. For instance, when the pack is close at him in cover, and he goes through the outside fence of the cover only, instead of going into the field, he drops down into the ditch, and every hound goes over him. The pack then make a swing outside, during which he crawls up the bank back again into cover, and gets probably to the other side before they cast back; by which time the scent, owing to the ground being stained, gets bad, and he has probably time to get fresher, and often steals away without being seen, as all the men are close to the hounds, with the belief that they will kill the next minute. But on these occasions, if the huntsman is awake, he will always order one of the whippers-in to remain at the opposite side of the cover. Independent of its being the best plan to kill a hunted fox, by sticking to the pack and cheering them in cover, it is the most likely means of making a fresh fox break cover, without any wide hounds getting on him, for it keeps the pack together, and makes any other foxes fly. Indeed it sometimes happens that the leading hounds kill their fox in cover, though not often, and then join the body of the pack, which are on a fresh one; which, unless a huntsman has kept his ear to, he is not aware of.

There is a wide difference of opinion, as to whether a large pack or a small one is best in large covers, where the object is to get away with one, or to make him fly or die. Although foxes are apt to hang in these covers it appears easy to prove that the smallest pack—say seventeen couple—has the advantage in many ways; and is more likely to make a fox fly, or kill him, than a pack of twenty-five or thirty couple. In the first place, a large cover generally holds more than one fox, often several; therefore, as a small pack is more likely to keep together when running in cover than a large one, there is less chance of changing, for it is impossible for a large pack to keep together long, when the ground is stained. The tail hounds have no scent to lead them on to keep pace with the forward hounds, consequently, when a little behind they cut across to get to them when they turn, and, in doing this, often cross the line of another fox; when, owing to there being so many hounds behind, they make so great a cry, that if it happens the leading hounds check at the time, it is ten to one but that they join the tail hounds, which would not have been the case if only one or two, or a few only, were running the fresh fox, as there would not have been such a crash. Consequently, when a fox is pressed so much, he will often fly; but had they once changed, it would have been different, and he would have stayed in cover probably; besides which, the ground is not so much stained, and also, by sticking to one, others find it best to get out of the way.

It often happens when a fox goes straight away for several miles a pretty good pace, it is evident from a sudden turn the hounds make that he is afraid to go on, and begins to head back. If, on occasions of this sort, he beats them out of scent and all hunting is at an end, the best plan is to finish with trotting back to the cover where he was found; most likely he will be got there, unless you go back with the hounds too quickly, for a fox often stops and listens when he finds he is not pressed, and should he hear the huntsman, or get wind of the pack on their way back, he will bear off, or lie down, which is one reason why he is not more easily beaten. If instead foxes were to go on straight, best pace, they could not stand it as they do, therefore it requires judgment in not getting back to the cover too quickly. This may be called, though unfairly so, lifting hounds; but it is not so, for it would not be done until every other cast had been made. The question therefore is this, if the hounds cannot hunt or feel a scent, will you adopt this plan, or go home? Some may say, neither, but go and find a fresh fox. By all means do this, if the pack have not done much and another can be found quickly; but in most countries it is easier said than done, and when doubtful, it is better to give the hounds this chance of recovering their first fox, or probably you may draw blank till nearly dark, and when you *have* found, all the men who were so very urgent for you to give up your first and find a fresh one, have left you to hunt alone, although you did it to oblige them, as your hounds had done a good day's work, instead of killing your first by perseverance. Besides, the recovery of a good fox in a brilliant run makes a good finish, and is enjoyed much more by every one than finding a second when horses are half tired. There is little chance of doing much with an afternoon fox, when the mettle is taken out of your pack in the morning; and a huntsman must take care not to beat his pack too often, or a repetition will make any pack slack.

When a huntsman is requested to draw for a second fox late in the day, it would be a fair question to put, "Gentlemen, we have had hard work lately, and have some distance home; but if I do find, will you promise not to leave me till it is finished?"

It is no uncommon thing to hear it said that halloos do more harm than good. This in some measure is quite true, and at times they are a great nuisance; but there are times when a man would give half he is worth for one, and then, when it is so valuable, few men have coolness enough to take the best means of profiting by it, by riding with his hounds up to the spot, and coolly, distinctly, and most deliberately inquiring where the fox was seen—*the identical spot*, if possible—which way he was going, where he came from, and how long since? For obvious reasons, the person who halloos is over-anxious to tell his tale, and if hurried will point out so-and-so, scarcely knowing what he is about. Besides this gives the hounds time to get their wind, and put their noses down, instead of flying beyond the scent, or taking the scent-heel; and if the time does not agree, which is often the case, though the question is not even asked, the huntsman can then leave it, and return; for by going off with the scent at once, he would be getting on one, either fresher or staler than that he was hunting. It must be a very young hand who has not found out this, but old heads forget it.

Also when a huntsman takes his hounds to a halloo, where a fox has crossed a ride in cover, he should, on ascertaining the spot, pull up ten or twelve paces before he gets to it, the hounds being at his horse's heels, and by turning his horse's head out of the road the same way the fox went, he will get them in on the side he wished; but had he ridden on quite to the spot, they were just as likely to take it heel as not, and more so, if the fox was going down wind. Simple as this plan is, many runs have been lost by not adopting it, for they may have taken the scent-heel through the whole side of the cover.

Much cheering and hallooing to hounds by a huntsman is generally disapproved of, but in large woodlands it keeps hounds together; sometimes it makes your hunted fox fly, and also is the cause of other foxes breaking another day, for they recollect it, and having got well off before, try it again. Few men have lungs to stand it, nor would they do it from choice, but the fact that hounds will come to a good shrill view-halloo quicker than to any horn in the world is beyond a doubt. Such is the effect of a real good cheer on hounds, that they actually jump round, so excited can they be made by it. Not so with a horn; it is true they will come to it, which is enough. If it is used frequently, it is thought by some to lose its effect on hounds. But in bad scenting countries, when it is necessary to cheer hounds a great deal to get them together, and to make them draw or hunt, the more assistance a man can get from his horn the better, or his voice cannot last if his constitution does; therefore he had better even use his horn occasionally in drawing to get hounds on, and to let them know where he is. It will also assist in moving a fox. By this method he will have voice left to halloo and cheer when they have found. This is only necessary in bad scenting countries, but in a good one no fear but all men have voice enough, and lucky indeed are they who do not require it, for it is mere play in comparison. Few men who hunt hounds in the north, know what a bad scenting country is. Let them ask Tom Sebright, one of the best, who now hunts Lord Fitzwilliam's hounds; as he once hunted part of Hampshire, the Hambledon country, half a season with Mr. Osbaldiston's hounds, he well knows the difference it made both to himself and his hounds,—so much so that no money would have kept him there, even had the hounds remained; for what is called in these lower countries a fair holding scent, in the upper countries they would call insufferable, and whip off and find a fresh fox. But if the same scent was to be always given up in the other cold-scenting country, they would not kill a fox in a month, and hounds might also as well be given up altogether.

Huntsmen are apt to think that their hunted fox must be more beaten than is the case, and often hang about at a check, trying every hedgerow, and expecting to see the hounds lay hold of him; but

M

it would be wiser, instead of dwelling so long, if they first made all their forward casts completely, and then came back. It certainly is no uncommon thing for a fox to lie down and be left behind altogether; and it has often happened that he has been found lying in a ditch, or some odd place, on the return of the hounds. But had he gone on during the time they were ferreting out all these places, it would probably be of little use afterwards if the hounds did hit off the scent.

It is no uncommon thing for a good fox, on his being first found, to go up wind for a mile or two, and then head short down wind, and never turn again. Probably instinct tells him that hounds will go such a pace up wind, that they will be a little blown, and that the change of scent down wind creates a slight check, which gives him the advantage.

Few things are so necessary for a huntsman to acquire as a thorough knowledge of the country he hunts. For to make a good cast when in difficulties, he should have a map of the country in his head. Unless he always knows the exact situation of the covers near during the chase, he cannot be prepared off-hand to make a proper cast, so as to take the narrowest parts between the covers; indeed he should be able to point with his hand direct to any cover named, let him be where he will, even if in the middle of a wood. It is truly remarkable how very few men appear to have thought this necessary.

These observations relating to huntsmen will nearly finish with one of the greatest consequence, which, though often unattended to, should be so most strictly, on the principle that whatever is worth doing at all is worth doing *well*. There is nothing more disheartening to a field of sportsmen, than for a huntsman or master of hounds to trifle with them—*pretending* to draw for a fox, when it is evident that they do not intend to let the hounds find one if they can help it—by taking them through the parts of a cover quickly where there is no lying, although there is plenty on the other side, which they avoid, knowing it would be a certain find if they would let the hounds draw it; or probably missing other sure places, and drawing unlikely ones, until their time is spun out that they may go home. This is an unpardonable trick. Why not at once say, We will go home, gentlemen? If this conduct proceeds from slackness in a huntsman, it is high time he should be drafted—his day is gone by. But, if there is any reason for his not wishing to find again, let him say so, and people will be satisfied, and go home without being disgusted. This seldom happens with men who hunt their own hounds, and it makes up for many deficiencies when men know that if sport is to be got, he will *try*, at all events; but every huntsman who has any head knows pretty well by the middle of the season where to put his hand on a fox (if there is one in the country), unless by accident it has been moved. If not, he is not half a huntsman.

Huntsmen, and men who keep hounds, are very apt to express themselves warmly on discovering that a fox has been injured, or if they think there has been an attempt to poison one, owing to his being mangy. But, if possible, they had better not express their thoughts, unless they can prove it and bring it home to the man, for nothing provokes a gentleman so much who does not hunt as to have it even hinted that his servants destroy foxes. It is a sort of reflection on a man's dignity to suppose that his servants would commit an act of this sort contrary to the master's wish. If there are grounds for suspicion, they had better not be stated openly, but represented by the master of the hounds, or some intimate friend of the gentleman, to whom every act of courtesy is due. Depend upon it, it is a mistaken notion that any man can be bullied into a thing of this sort; for although he may apparently give way to the wishes of numbers, yet no man forgets that he has been treated harshly.

Deer are often the cause of much trouble to a huntsman with a pack of fox-hounds, and although he may flatter himself that he has got the steadiest pack possible, the most trifling accident may make them otherwise. And young hounds cannot be taken too often amongst deer during the summer before they are entered, and they should not be taken out to exercise with the old hounds till just before cub-hunting, if they are at all before that begins, by which time they ought to be tolerably handy and thoroughly used to see riot. But the following account of an accident with the writer's pack will probably be sufficient to make others more cautious. At the end of the summer in the month of August, when the writer was from home, his men, to save trouble, unknown to him took out the young hounds with the old ones to exercise, and were passing through a park full of deer, where they had constantly been all the summer without having shown the slightest sign of riot. On going through some fern a young hare jumped up, and some of the young hounds took after her, directly into a herd of deer. The men foolishly rode after them, rating them at the same time. This set the deer running, and with them the young hounds, and by hallooing to them some of the two-and three-year hunters broke away. This caused them to halloo more, so that at last the whole pack joined, but fortunately did not pull one down before they were got away. The writer, on hearing of, it came home, took them out cub-hunting earlier than usual; and on the first day, having killed a brace of cubs after running *six hours incessantly,* ventured to take them amongst the deer. At first they were quiet, but at length a young hound broke away, and shortly afterwards two-thirds of the pack. They were with difficulty stopped, then tied up to the park pales and flogged, about fifty in a row, till all hands were tired. A few days after all the most vicious were taken there by themselves in couples, or rather three together; but this was of no use, they soon broke away and were punished. This continued for six weeks from daybreak till the afternoon, by which time every hound was perfectly steady. Amongst other plans, a deer was constantly put in the kennel for several hours every day, and if a hound looked at it, he was rated or punished. A few of the very worst were drafted, but the pack was never steadier than during the season after it; and although great part of the cub-hunting was lost, they killed more foxes than any other season that the writer kept hounds. This trouble was bad enough, but it was still worse to be told on all sides at the time that it would be impossible ever to break them, or to hunt the forest or where deer were again. By many this would have been believed, but having fortunately heard it stated by one of the best sportsmen some years before, that he used to hunt with Mr. Land, who kept hounds at Hambledon, and hunted the forest of Brere just before it was enclosed, and whose hounds used to hunt both deer and fox at different seasons of the year—that is, the deer during the summer, and fox during the winter—in *the same forest;* and the writer has since been credibly informed from others in that country that, after a week or fortnight hunting fox, they were as steady to fox as if they had never hunted deer, which were now constantly crossing them. But it is fair and right to add, that in those days this gentleman did not enter so many young hounds, and these were not entered till the fox-hunting season began, and of course, did not hunt deer till the following summer.

The following is a sketch of a general cast, made by the writer for many years. Although the principle of it, at starting, is startling, yet few succeed better, namely, that of first holding the hounds the way he *does not think* the fox is gone. Thus, when at a check and the pack have made their own swing, he then holds them round to the right or left, whichever is most up wind, consequently this side would have been the most unlikely, for they probably would not have checked at first had it been right, owing to its being rather up wind; when, if it does happen to be right, they hit it off directly, so that it takes scarcely a minute to hold them round back, behind the spot where they checked, about a hundred yards or so. He then turns and takes a little wider circle back, round in front all the way, to the left the same distance, till he reaches or nearly so, the line he came to behind the check at first. Now having ascertained for certain that his fox is not gone back, or short to the right or left, he can with confidence begin a wider cast than he would have ventured to make otherwise, owing to a fear that the fox had headed back, or to the right or left. The wide cast he commences on the left from behind, progressing according to his judgment, and selecting the best scenting-ground forward beyond any fallow or bad scenting-ground. As he now knows that the fox must be gone on,

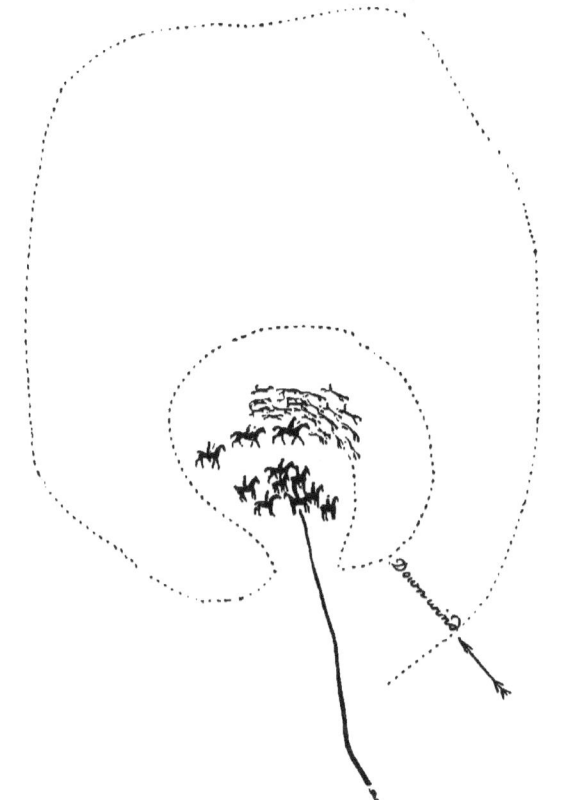

T. Smith, Esq., del.

SKETCH OF A CAST.

Facing page 168.

this cast is continued all round in front, and to the right, till he again reaches the line behind. He then takes a wider cast either way, and is guided by circumstances; but nineteen times out of twenty this last is not required, except the fox is headed some distance back, and the steam and stain of the horses prevents the hounds feeling the scent, the quick first cast back. If there is no wind to guide him, there may be a cover to which the fox is gone, on the left; but still he holds them first the unlikely side.

Sheep are often great enemies to fox-hunting, more particularly in the upper, or rather the grass countries; but if a huntsman keeps his eyes open, this obstacle to sport can be much lessened. For if a fox crosses a field in which sheep are, as they are quick-sighted and timid, they invariably show by the situation of some of them that they have been frightened; and some will be seen in a line with their heads all the same way, or they will form a line all across the field, with their heads in an opposite direction to the part where the fox passed, which part will be clear of sheep. But it also sometimes happens that young sheep, after a fox has gone by, follow his line to the spot where he went through the fence. It should also be borne in mind that a fox is not likely to be headed by sheep, as he is in the constant habit of crossing through sheep at night, which is proved by the tracks in snow. Consequently, a huntsman will do well, generally, to hold his hounds on beyond the sheep as soon as they have made their own swing; nor deviate from this, even when there is a good scent, for on these days the scent of the sheep and cattle is equally stronger,—one cause for the assertion that the scent in these countries is over-rated.

In order to remove the obstruction (that of sheep), in Leicestershire a plan has been proposed, which, if adopted, may be of some avail—namely, to raise a fund for the purpose of paying the farmers who are willing to allow their shepherds to pen their sheep in a corner, or part of a field, instead of being spread all over it, from about half-past eleven till three or four o'clock, for a certain distance round the place of meeting. Few remedies are without objections: and to this there may be some. In the first place, the shepherds who are to do this will probably have dogs; at all events they will be about, where before they were not, and will be looking out for the fox, etc. Where shepherds have dogs it is found to be a great nuisance: so much so, that a celebrated sportsman in the south has, it is said, adopted the plan of paying the shepherds a certain sum every day the hounds meet near, to keep their dogs fastened up,—this being a very open country, where dogs are of great use to the shepherds.

Blank days will seldom happen if a country is hunted regularly and without partiality. It is the too frequently hunting favourite covers, and neglecting to hunt the outskirts, which is one cause of blank days. The foxes go where they are quietest: and the consequence is they are unfairly destroyed, on the plea that it is no use to keep foxes if they are not hunted. And to ensure sport, a man must be very judicious in making his appointments, so as not to draw the same cover too often, although pretty sure of finding. And it is best not to name the fixtures until the end of the week, for the week following, as it is impossible to say which covers will not be disturbed. And few, besides large-holding covers, will bear drawing oftener than once in three weeks, to be a tolerably sure find. And that country, also, generally shows the best sport where the outskirts are fairly hunted, equally with the best parts of it, without regard to distance, because the foxes go straighter, and vary the line of the runs. The wildest and best will go where they can be most quiet, which is generally in the most distant covers, and, when found, go back into the best country.

But there are stout foxes which will not leave the covers they are used to, beyond a few days; and constantly run the same line when found. Such require extraordinary methods to beat them; and the following account of a run may be a useful hint.

An old fox had been found several times by the pack belonging to the present writer, and as invariably run a ring of about three miles, taking a round of small covers; by which he generally moved other foxes, and saved himself. Application was made late in the season to try one more day for this fox, as he was suspected of doing mischief amongst game. He was found, as usual, and run the same ring twice, When running it the third time, the hounds were stopped, and quietly walked back, to the surprise of a large field of sportsmen; on reaching an open part, as was expected, the hunted fox was seen coming the same line as before, directly towards the hounds, which got a view, and so astonished him, that he went straight away, and was killed twelve miles (as the crow flies) from where he was found.

When hounds have a long distance to cover, beyond ten or twelve miles, it is advisable to send them on overnight; on which occasions, the next day, they certainly show themselves to greater advantage, as they are more light, lively, and fitter to go, than when only a short time out of the kennel, or when turned out of an omnibus.

It is a disadvantage to a pack not hunting four days a week, because, when they hunt only three,—there are many hounds which seldom hunt two days together,—they do not get acquainted with each other's tongues to have that confidence which generally makes them fly together at once, but will stop and listen to the stranger, till they hear hounds they know to be true.

Cub-Hunting

It is a mistake to put off cub-hunting till late in the autumn, when the intention of it is to reserve the foxes till the season begins, particularly in game countries. Some men are content to let a whipper-in go round with the keeper to be shown a litter of cubs, which being done, they have a present made; but it is a great chance if the cubs are ever seen afterwards. The hounds had better go once round to every doubtful litter, as early as they possibly can for the corn,—and even before it is cut, if a whipper-in by standing on that side can keep them back out of the corn. Few men are half sufficiently aware of the great necessity of moving foxes that are known of, by a day's cub-hunting. They are not easily found by fox-takers afterwards, or by keepers, for they beat out from home after they have travelled a little in consequence of being disturbed, etc.

It is necessary in the hot weather in September to go out cub-hunting as soon as it is light, and if it can be over by eight or nine o'clock so much the better. By way of change the writer has tried it in the afternoon instead, leaving the kennel probably at four o'clock, and commencing about five or six in the evening, which makes it a more agreeable job than getting up in the middle of the night. The cubs are by that time moving, and soon found; and the longer you run the cooler it is, instead of getting broiled with heat at nine or ten in the morning. The result was, the cubs took more time to kill than in the morning; probably owing to their being more fit to run, being lighter. But the later it was, the cooler it was also; and, consequently, the hounds were never so much distressed as in the heat of the morning, which increased as the hounds got tired. Yet however agreeable it may be, it is not so much like business as in the morning: the men have a great deal to do afterwards, and it disarranges the establishment. Still it is a more gentlemanlike hour for a man who hunts his own hounds: and on a quiet evening nothing can exceed the pleasurable feeling it creates. One of the greatest objections to it is, that many men are induced to ride out at that time with the hounds, who would not early in the morning: and nothing is more annoying to a huntsman than having strange horses in the rides when the young hounds first enter, and the pack are running in cover. It cuts them off and prevents their getting about with the huntsman, and they get ridden over, either owing to their own awkwardness or that of the horse or rider. Therefore it is best not to make known when they are going: at all events, unless those who do go out, go with the understanding that they are not to expect sport, or get in the way of the hounds. They will be apt to urge a huntsman to have a gallop, which would be as childish in him to do, as for them to ask of him: for probably if he did he would lose half his young hounds, and all the benefit to them of cub-hunting. Although the writer is not aware that this plan has ever been adopted by any other person, he is bold enough to assert that it is a good one, and beyond all doubt most agreeable.

CHAPTER II

WHIPPER-IN

TO be a whipper-in requires both a good eye and a good ear: but the greatest qualification for one is that he should be free from conceit, so that he will consider it right to obey the huntsman most implicitly, whether he thinks him right or wrong, and not hesitate, but at once and instantly do what is required: then he does his duty, but not till then. Even if he has reason to know that what the huntsman is going to do is wrong, in making a cast, etc., and that he could put him right, he will gain his point sooner by more quickly turning the hounds to him, with this sort of feeling in his own mind, "Try your own way as quickly as you can, and then try mine"; for what is the use of *his* thinking, when the *hounds* are going with the huntsman?

It is necessary that a whipper-in should be naturally fond of the sport, so that his heart and soul are in it. Even men who hunt with hounds, if they are really fond of it, cannot help occasionally showing a wish to assist and whip in. And men who have hunted their own hounds have often felt a wish to become whippers-in, knowing, as they do, that it is possible for a good whipper-in to do more towards the sport on most days than the huntsman. The thing is, to find a man who does not wish to save himself; and if he is really fond of it, he never will. This point found out, decides whether he keeps his place or not; for they are apt to take it too quietly, forgetting that the first exertion may save their lungs, their limbs, and body, during the whole season afterwards. Indeed, *some* say that a whipper-in is not worth keeping if, after a hound has thrown his tongue twice in cover or riot, he does not instantly get to him, through bushes or what not, either on or off his horse, and correct the hound on the spot—if possible get hold of him by the tail, and lay the whip along his side, rating him by name at the same time. He will be so frightened as well as hurt, that he will not readily forget it;

and the rest of the pack will recollect it also, and know the rate, and that it does not go for nothing, and fly at a word: thus—"Ga-a-t away! Des-pe-rate! ga-a-t away, ga-a-t away! you-on, you-on! cup, cup!" But instead of this, when the hounds are running riot, they are often desperately exerting themselves by standing up in their stirrups and bawling, "War hare, war hare! get on there! get away!" which, besides being of no use, the young hounds get so used to hear it, that they take no notice of it; and at a distance, say the other side of the cover, is mistaken by men and hounds, too, for a view-halloo. Hounds are often seen listening to it, and men even often call out, "Hark! halloo!" And when these clever fellows fancy they know the hounds that were guilty of riot, and see them in the open probably half an hour afterwards, they ride at them, intending to cut them in two almost, when they either hit or ride over some other hound; and even when they hit the right, the hound does not know what it was for. But one often sees another foolish thing done. When hounds are at a check or cold-hunting, a whipper-in has not till then been able to get at a hound which has been running riot, and takes the opportunity to give him a cut; the consequence is, that the cry of this hound will instantly make the hunting hounds throw up their heads toward it, and often they do not get their noses down again in a hurry. Indeed, some sly old hounds will drop their sterns, give a sniff as much as to say, "Fool, hunt it yourself!"

It is a good plan when any particular hound or hounds are fond of riot—such as deer or hare—on approaching near the spot where either of these are likely to jump up, for one of the whips to get off his horse slyly, and walk by the side, then when he sees the hound prick up his ears, or show the least inclination to take notice of either riot, to give him a proper good stroke with his whip, or probably he may be off after the deer or hare, and lead away the whole pack.

Nothing is more common, when a view-halloo is heard, than to hear the whipper-in, when sitting quietly on his horse, calling out, "Hark, halloo! hark, halloo!" instead of *instantly* getting to the hounds, which are probably hanging on some stale scent or up wind, and then rating sharply with, "Hark, halloo! get away! get away"! with a smack of his whip; and this is done in a tenth part of the time—indeed much less generally; besides the service he has done this way. Had he stopped away at a distance and hallooed, he would have prevented the hounds hearing the halloo, and would be doing actual mischief.

But a whipper-in has often opportunities of assisting in getting hounds to a halloo when getting to them, without rating, which would be of no use. It is when a halloo is heard down wind, and the hounds cannot hear it. If the huntsman is not there, he had better cap them on, till they are within hearing of the halloo, then pull up, and let them pass with a "Hark, halloo!" But some men will ride back to the hounds, and, forgetting that they cannot hear it, begin rating and smacking their whips to no purpose; except that it makes it still more difficult for the hounds to hear the halloo.

If a halloo is heard at a distance by the whipper-in, and neither the huntsman nor hounds hear it, when at a check, he had better get half-way between the halloo and the hounds, and then halloo himself, till the hounds or huntsman come; for if he went all the way to the halloo there would be the same chance of *his* not being heard also.

If a whipper-in views a fox, on the opposite side of the cover to the huntsman or not, he should most distinctly halloo—either "Tally-ho back," or, "Tally-ho away"—to let the huntsman and field know which it is, instead of merely hallooing "Tally-ho," which is often the case.

As soon as, or before, if possible, hounds are thrown into a large cover, to draw it, one whipper-in should clap on down wind as fast as he can, in case a good fox steals away, as the first that goes is generally the best. But if only one whip, this one will be better employed the early part of the season (till Christmas) in keeping near the hounds, as the young ones will be apt to run riot, and until this time two whips are better than one. But if they have been active up to this time, one whipper-in the remainder of the season is generally all that is required. The surest way to get a run before December is to take every method to get away with the first fox that breaks cover. When in the chase, and the hounds are going through a large cover, if there are two whips out, the first should not follow the huntsman if there is another ride equally likely, or nearly so; the other whip should go the line the huntsman does, in case of accidents.

A whipper-in should not ride as if he was riding for amusement or credit, but should have his eye to the hounds without distressing his horse, which is a great recommendation to every master of hounds. The greatest fools generally ride the hardest; the proof of their being so, is that they forget they must go on till night, but men who hunt with hounds only can go home when they please. A proof of a clever whipper-in is, that he is always up at a check, without ever being seen in front except by accident, and no one else there; but it is his duty to hold in, and by that means he has always something left in his horse when others are beaten. There are whippers-in now going who are never seen in a quick thing, and yet are never missed, because they are always up when wanted. Who looks for a whipper-in, except then? He does not hunt the fox. And if he has a good eye and ear, with a knowledge of the country, by keeping within sight, or hearing, takes advantage of every turn of the hounds, and saves much distance and severe ground. Nor is it fair to abuse a whipper-in for not being with hounds on all occasions, particularly when the huntsman is very quick; for there are some who handle their hounds, and get about so quickly, that if the whip had only to follow him without looking after a hound, he would have enough to do to keep with him. In short, with a quick huntsman, if this allowance was not made, even a real good whip would soon lose his character in the opinion of many who do not understand it, which makes it desirable to have a second whip in countries where appearances are much considered; though, as before stated, a second whip is rarely wanted after Christmas, for when the scent is so good as to run clean away from a good whip, who has stopped, probably, merely to turn a hound, he is not wanted until a check, and by that time he is up.

The great use of two whips is when hounds divide and one lot goes away, then the first should stop back and bring on the other lot as soon as he can, the nearest way. The second whip should go on, and keep within sight of the huntsman, to be at his command to turn the hounds to him, etc.

If hounds are running a fox through, or in a small cover near a large one, the whip should clap back between the two covers to prevent the fox from going into the large one, and should stop there till the hounds have gone on; and, if it is early in the season, what riot there is will be the side next the large cover, and will probably cross into it, and he will be there to stop a young hound.

When a whipper-in is behind, bringing on hounds in the chase, he should be careful not to halloo them on when passing a cover, but get them on quietly, by capping, if necessary, or he will move a fresh fox. He will do well to stop and listen occasionally, to ascertain which way the pack is bearing; and by noticing the hounds that are with him, he will often discover it, although he himself could not hear the cry, and by so doing he will frequently save much distance and hard riding.

It is a good old fashion for a whipper-in to have a stirrup leather buckled across his shoulder, in case of accidents; and always to have a pair of couples to his saddle. Also, to carry a lancet, and a bottle of sharp water, for cuts and overreaches, to be applied as soon as seen, viz.,

> Eight drops of oil of thyme.
> Ten drops of oil of vitriol.
> One ounce of spirits of wine.

It is a good plan to have a feather stuck into the cork of the phial, with the light end of the feather downwards; it is then always ready to be used, and there is not the chance of losing the contents when using it. The writer has made use of this receipt for many years with the greatest success, in overreaches particularly, which (if it is applied immediately, and three or four times a day) will become dry, a crust will form over the injured part, and it will not prevent the horse from working. Every stable should have a bottle of it ready.

CHAPTER III

SPORTSMAN

Better to hunt the fields for health unbought,
Than fee the doctor for a nauseous draught.

ALL men who are fox-hunters are not sportsmen; and that some even wish not to be thought so, the following anecdote may prove. In the year 182— the writer was staying at Melton during the season, with only a short stud of hunters and a hack of his own, besides what he hired. As may be supposed, he never thought of seeing a second run with the hounds the same day. On one occasion, having seen a good fox killed, he merely stopped to see the second found, and then went home. Some time during the afternoon he met two men, well known in the hunt, who had gone the second run, and inquired of them if they had killed their second fox; but neither of them knew, although they came home part of the way with the hounds. This was mentioned to the master of the pack next day, and the reply was: "You may not be aware of it, but many men here would consider it an insult to be supposed to know anything about it. Had you asked them who had gone best during the run, you would have had a story as long as your arm." He then told the fact, that the second fox was killed.

Another circumstance, amongst many others, occurred at the close of the season, 183—, confirming the assertion that the pleasure of many men of the present day consists only in riding. A party after dinner were discussing, not the merits of one of the best runs of the season, but a point *now* of greater consequence, the merits of the horses, etc. The question was asked, Who had the best of it? Some man's name was given, and also the name of the second best; on which a man, who had been attentively listening, and who had been with the hounds on the day in question, immediately exclaimed, "Then by G—d I'll sell my horses, and give it up; for I'll swear that I had the best of it throughout that run!" etc. And he actually did send his twelve hunters to Tattersall's shortly afterwards, and they were sold. It is fair to add that this gentleman was oftener first than any other man throughout the run alluded to.

According to the above, enough has been said to prove that many men do not care about hunting; but the present rage for steeple-chases will give those men an opportunity of distinguishing themselves by desperate riding; and when they learn that they are outdone by horse-dealers, grooms, etc., it is probable that they may think more of the *hunting* part of the day's sport. These hints are written with the hope that already some young ones may be coming on to whom they may be useful.

First, it is necessary to go to the place of meeting; and in doing this it is suggested that men should avoid passing through a cover which is likely to be drawn that day, for a good fox is always awake, and on hearing horses near, will often leave his kennel and steal away. The consequence is that a good day's sport is converted into a bad one; for on drawing this cover, the hounds get on the stale scent of this fox which is gone, and hunt a walking pace for some time, probably over a fine country, instead of going away on good terms with him; and they may afterwards find a bad fox when they ought to be going home.

On arriving at the place of meeting, men had better say all they have to say to the master of the hounds, or to the huntsman; for if they attempt it after they have thrown off, they may fancy they have not been treated with common civility. Nothing is more annoying than for either of these, particularly the huntsman, to feel obliged to answer questions of any sort after throwing off; for although he may appear not to have anything on his mind, he either is, or ought to be, thinking how to show a good day's sport. For instance, he has just drawn a cover blank, and is waiting for a hound or two left back, or some other cause, and appears then to be at leisure to talk or answer questions: not so, his mind is, or ought to be, occupied in thinking which is the next cover likely, which the best way to it, so as to get the wind, and at the same time to enable him to get to the best laying in it for his fox; or he may be considering how such or such a hound behaves, whether fond of riot, or what not; or waiting to give some order to the whipper-in. No huntsman is free to think of anything else; and therefore, when any person asks him a question, he must not be surprised if he does not get a correct answer. Nothing is more often done, or more unfair, than to ask him where he is going to next after drawing one cover, for many circumstances may occur to induce him to change. After having told some person, for instance, just as he arrives at the cover-side he hears that some people are shooting, or have been that day with all sorts of dogs, or he may draw a hedgerow, or a small cover in his way, which he did not think worth speaking of; and if the person told has told others, and they have gone on, and afterwards find that the hounds have slipped away with their fox, they blame the huntsman. Therefore men had better depend entirely on themselves, and never lose sight of the hounds either before they have found or afterwards, if they can keep near enough, particularly in windy weather; for this is the only sure and safe plan. Many men go great distances to cover, and, owing to not attending to it frequently lose the best of the run at first, and have to distress their horses beyond recovery in getting up to the hounds, and cannot enjoy what little remains of the run, and often are not lucky enough to get up at all. And there are days, though unfortunately not frequent, that as soon as hounds are thrown into cover they find, and get together like magic, and away without scarcely a hound throwing tongue; when, even if a man is present, it is ten to one (if the cover is a large one) against his getting away well with them, unless he adopts the plan of trying never to lose sight of them. It is true the loss of a run of this sort ought to be a caution, for it is owing to a burning scent that there is scarcely any cry—it is the pace which stops the music.

If hounds are drawing a large cover, and cannot be seen, never let them get out of hearing. To prevent which, the only certain way is to keep down wind, and the huntsman must be heard; this plan should be adopted, even if it is much farther round. It is not here meant that a man should gallop off all round a cover down wind, but get on steadily opposite the hounds; or by getting too forward, he might head back a fox, and thereby be the cause of a bad run instead of a good one. Had the men stood still when down wind, or out of sight, a good fox might have gone away, and the first which breaks cover is likely to be the best: but he being headed, owing to thoughtless riders, the hounds may change to a bad one, and run the cover for hours until he is killed. If these men only knew how much they were abused for not attending to this, and would recollect the difference of a good run and a bad one, they would act differently.

If it happens that a man views a fox breaking cover, he should not halloo until he is got away some distance, nearly, or quite across, a good-sized field; for if he halloos too soon the fox will head back into cover. The following plan will save much trouble. If the fox is gone away, to halloo "Tally-ho away!" or, "Tally-ho, awawoy!" this being more easy to halloo loudly. If the fox heads back into cover, halloo "Tally-ho back!" or "boick!" the halloo to be distinctly given, in order that the huntsman and the men on the other side of the cover should know whether the fox is gone away or headed back. But if he only halloos "Tally-ho!" which is too commonly the case, the huntsman and the rest of the field suppose that he (the fox) is gone away, and gallop round the cover, some one way and some another, to the halloo. When they get there, they find the fox is gone back: the consequence of which is, not only, that they have ridden their horses for nothing, but that, in coming round, they have probably headed the fox again; when had they stood still on hearing that the halloo was back, the fox would have gone away at some other point. Some foxes that would fly at first get shy and frightened by hallooing, and though stout and equal to any, never leave the cover alive; and if a gentleman has headed him back, he has the blessing of the whole field.

Or, if a man sees a fox cross a ride in cover, if he halloos at all, which he ought to do if the hounds are at check, it should be, "Tally-ho, yoi over!" which is sufficient to let the huntsman know that the fox has crossed the ride. And when a man has viewed a fox and has given a view-halloo, he had better remain perfectly quiet, and not try to get another view elsewhere; all he gets for his pains is that he is accused of trying to prevent a fox breaking cover; and certain it is, that though he may not try to do it, he by this does all he can to prevent it, and gets blamed accordingly for having probably spoiled a good day's sport.

A man's love of hunting, independent of riding, has been estimated, though unfairly, at times by simply remarking his having no thong to his whip. Although it may be unjust to say that such men are not sportsmen, yet, as it happens to every man some time during a season to see a fox break cover and head back, while he is the only person there or near at the time, if he should not have a thong to his whip he has no means of stopping the pack, which come out of cover, and flash half, or probably all the way, across the field, when, had he had a whip to smack, he could have turned them back at once, and have prevented the fox from gaining probably half an hour's advantage, by slipping away on the other side of the cover. When men see that their own sport may be injured by this fashion, it does appear most strange that it should have been adopted, much more continued, unless it really is to show their indifference to the sport; bringing with it, as it does, the chance of running over many a hound which may happen to be in the way of their horses; and, after having ridden over it, they will call out, " Ware horse!" when, in fact, it ought to have been, "Ware hound!" and the hound is ruined, because the gentleman did not choose to ride with a hunting-whip.

It sometimes happens that a hound in the chase crosses a horse in his gallop, or slips through a fence, and under a horse when taking a jump, and the hound is killed. This certainly may be called an accident. The owner and huntsman, of course, are much annoyed and irate at the moment; but they cannot blame a man for it as in the other case, when a smack of a whip would have saved it, but well knowing, as they must do, that it was done in the ardour of the chase; and many masters would rather witness such accidents occasionally than see men hunting without that ardent feeling for sport. Deprive fox-hunting of that intoxicating sensation, and it becomes wretchedly spiritless, and men may as well hunt a tame rabbit round a drawing-room, with the dread of being called to order for fear of breaking the crockery. No! Fox-hunting is no longer what it should be, when men ride in dread of being overhauled or abused by a master or a huntsman, who cannot himself ride at the head; for when he is there (in his place) and can look the men in the face, he is sure to be obeyed at a word; and it is difficult, or impossible, to instil into men who do not understand hunting, or scarcely even when hounds are at a check, the exact distance they ought to keep from hounds.

It often happens that young men are observed to take every opportunity of giving their horses a gallop before the hounds have found their fox; and indeed it often happens that their horses are more than half beaten before that time, although others at the same time are perfectly fresh after the hounds have been drawing several hours. Not long since, a young man from one of the universities amused a party who overheard him asking the whipper-in to follow him over a gate merely for amusement, whilst the hounds were drawing in a contrary direction; but he had that pleasure to himself. The hounds shortly afterwards found and had a good run. This gentleman went well for five or ten minutes, but was not seen or heard of afterwards that day; his horse was beaten before the fox was found.

There is an old saying, that "It is a bad wind that blows no good"; and, however much it is to be regretted that men do not enter into the real sport of fox-hunting as formerly, there is this advantage, that men are not constantly speaking to hounds, or cheering them by name,—a thing scarcely ever done in the present day, though it is reported to have been a common occurrence in the last century,— and the extraordinary quickness with which hounds get together may be attributed to this cause. It is not meant here that huntsmen never wish to see gentlemen lend assistance, for the huntsman to even the best appointed packs are at times glad of any one who will turn a hound, and by so doing get his warmest thanks; for it has probably been the means of finishing a good run well, when even one minute lost would have made all the difference in the scent. But that assistance is out of the power of forward riders who have *no thong* to their whip, and although one smack of it would be invaluable, they cannot make use of it.

It is not the intention of the writer to dwell much on the subject of riding to hounds; but the rage for it has become so great, that many men do not look before they leap, therefore the following fact may be useful. About the year 1835, a gentleman was riding well with the Hambledon hounds in Hampshire, and when they were going best pace, he naturally put his horse at the lowest place in the fence, and the next moment found himself on his back, and his horse out of sight; when, on rising from the ground, he was not a little startled at seeing a well, or rather a draw-hole the size of a well, into which his horse had gone headlong, and was dashed to pieces; as was the case with the saddle. The fall was of considerable depth; it was a place from which chalk had been excavated to manure the land. The writer once hunted that country, and recollects three hounds being lost for three days, and were found in a well of this description; but they were all got out alive and saved. This, and the fact of his having seen men when riding jealously go headlong into a pond on the other side of the fence, and on one occasion into a chalk-pit, he thinks may even make a steeple-chaser look before he leaps; for he should recollect that no one has marked out his line with hounds as in a steeplechase.

One of the first things for a man to acquire in riding to hounds is, an eye to hounds; that is, in chase always to keep his eye on the leading hound, which he will easily distinguish from the pack by observing that the moment the leading hound (or hounds, but generally only one) catches the scent, he drops his stern as straight as a tobacco-pipe, and the stern of the other hound which had it the moment before will rise. It often happens that several get it when the scent is pretty good; and if so, it will be easier to see it. By observing this, he turns his horse's head as he sees the hounds turn, and gains a great advantage over those men who only look at the body of the pack, and who go beyond where it is necessary for their horse to go. A man with a good eye to hounds will beat others who have not, although much better mounted than himself, and at times save his horse much distance and deep ground.

If men would pay attention to the cry of hounds when running in cover, instead of riding in to the end of the ride, without listening, merely because

"One fool, it is said, makes many."

when they started the hounds were going in that direction, they would often save their horses much work; for, on listening, they would find that the hounds had turned in another direction. One fool, it is said, makes many; and it is no uncommon thing to see one man start off, and a whole string of horses follow without knowing why, and have to return after going all through the wood. A very little trouble and patience will teach any man which way hounds are turning in cover; and he will find it a great saving and advantage to his horse and himself too. It is true, that old sportsmen beat men of the present day; *they* were properly entered to fox-hunting, and were taught to depend on their own eyes and ears. For instance, a fox after a run gets to a large cover, where there is an earth stopped at the farther end, or the country is too open to make it probable that the fox will face it, he (the old sportsman), when he reaches the cover, quietly pulls up, and keeps his ear to the hounds, going on steadily; by which his horse gets his wind, the fox does head, finding the earth stopped, etc., and the hounds bring him round back to the old sportsman. But during this whole time the hard riders have been going best pace much farther than the hounds, which by this time have left the cover, and returning the way they came with only the old one with them; and this because he was the only man who kept his ear to them.

Nothing shows ignorance in the field so much as not getting out of the way when the huntsman is coming past with the hounds, particularly at a check in a road. Men appear to forget that they cannot hunt without the pack. If it is in a road or in cover, it is most necessary, or the hounds must break out of the road into the cover, and possibly cross the line of another fox, and bring back the rest of the pack, which the huntsman is getting on.

Most men are aware that a skirting hound is considered a great enemy to sport, but a decided skirting rider does almost as much mischief. It is true he may say he goes out to please himself, and to ride as he likes best, but he must not forget that he has no excuse for spoiling the sport of others, and, although he is not abused to his face, he is behind his back. A story is told of a good old sportsman who was often annoyed by some men for not acting as he thought right in the field, and the only method he had of correcting them was by taking an opportunity, when the whipper-in was also committing the same fault, of heartily cursing *him* in their presence, finishing with "I may d—n *you!*"

Men who are not acquainted with the grass countries, in particular where the fences consist of live quicks and thorns, will do well to notice when a hedge is cut which way it is laid down to the top, and put his horse at it obliquely, with his head *from* the root of the thorn, and the top of the thorn being weak will give way to the horse's legs; but if he goes straight against it, he stands a good chance of a fall,—and if he goes obliquely, on the contrary plan, he reduces his fall to a certainty should the horse not clear any strong plasher which rises when the horse's knees are under it,—but not so the other way.

Young sportsmen are apt to think it right to be first if they can throughout a run; but they will do well to take it quietly at the beginning, and by that means they may be first at the end of the run, which otherwise they would never have seen—particularly if it is a good one, and if so, it will be a feather in his cap. A real good run seldom occurs, and when it does, it is seldom duly appreciated; for to get one requires so many circumstances combined—first, a good fox, then a good find and a good scent, then a good country, good luck, etc. The chances against it are innumerable—a bad scent, bad fox, bad find, not getting well away with him, and a hundred accidental circumstances to bring them to a check, without being overridden. The fox is headed by an old woman, or even a child of four years old may spoil a run; a dog, pig, sheep, cattle, cross-roads, false halloos, changing foxes—in short, no end to chances. But when there is not a good scent, more mischief is done by overriding than by all the other obstacles together; and it is much to be regretted that all men will not learn when hounds throw up, that is, when they throw up their noses at a check, which a man must either be blind not to see, or is afraid some other man will ride by him. And there are men who *will* pass the first man when he pulls up at a check, and they are the men who do the mischief—on whom the huntsman or master of the hounds should keep an eye. The first man forces on amongst the hounds at a check, and drives them beyond it; when up come lots of horses, smoking like steam-engines, on the very spot where the hounds first threw up, and where the fox headed or turned short to the right or left probably; then, instead of appearing to be aware that they have caused the check, like at the building of the tower of Babel, there begins a confusion of tongues, instead of each being anxiously quiet, with the hope of not attracting the hounds by a word even, of so much consequence is it just then; forgetting that by prolonging the check—which talking is likely to do—they throw away the advantages they have gained by being in the first flight, and give the rest of the field time to get up.

Those men get on best with hounds in a sharp run who always follow them through covers, even if there is no ride, if possible. Unless a man has been used to a woodland country, and has allowed his horse to have his head, and to pick his own way through a new-cut wood, stubs, etc., he had better keep the track; but if a man has nerve enough to allow his horse to have his nose down to his knees, and never to guide him through stubs, the horse will not lame himself. The fact is, the horse will be looking at one stub, and the man at another; so that when the horse is guided from where *he* was looking and intended to step, it is an even chance but that he knocks his legs to pieces.

Some years since a master of hounds, who hunted them himself, paid the writer a visit at the end of the season, and brought four hunters. He came determined to see everything that happened during each day's sport, and followed the writer everywhere through cover, etc., who soon observed to him that he would knock his horse's legs to pieces if he did not keep the road through a newly-cut wood, because he did not allow his horse to have his head, but was constantly pulling him one way or the other, consequently the horse was blundering against the stubs all the time. It is needless to add the fact that, at the end of the first week, not one horse of the four could go out of the stable, owing to their legs being so bruised and swollen, although others which went over the same ground had legs as clean as a foal's.

A man who hunts with another man's hounds should open his eyes and ears, but shut his mouth, or he will be likely to have this question put to him, if nothing worse, "Pray, sir, who made you huntsman?"

It may be useful for young sportsmen to know that when a fox goes up wind at first, he will often go a mile or two, and then head back down wind; therefore, if he is not first, his horse will be the better for his not having pressed him; and if the fox keeps on up wind, he is not likely to be thrown out, as he will be sure to hear them, and be able to get to them afterwards.

Nothing is more common, though most absurd, than for men who reside in a particular quarter in a hunting country to confine themselves to the meets of the hounds in that quarter, although they meet often quite as near, or nearer, and in a better country, probably the other side of some road, which is this person's boundary. It is true they know that country better; but surely to men who can ride, the wilder and stranger a country is the more it is like fox-hunting. It is the doubtful feeling when a fox is found, not knowing where you will be the next ten minutes, that makes fox-hunting so different from all other sports. Men who really like sport had better go ten miles to meet hounds in a good country, than two in a bad one.

When men have favourite horses they do not like to run any risk by sending them on over-night from fifteen to twenty miles, but prefer sending them on early in the morning; which is certainly an odd way of showing their regard, for on no occasion can it happen but that a good inn is to be found near the place of meeting, and surely there can be no hesitation whether to choose a horse which has been travelling three or four hours, or one fresh out of the stable, even if the groom did start very early in the morning,—say four o'clock,—and in the hunting season there is much doubt whether he would start so soon by two hours probably, so that the horse has often no time to get fresh. All that can be said is, that this practice is penny wise and pound foolish.

So in respect to riding a hunter home, probably twenty or twenty-five miles or more, after a hard day's work with hounds. Let the day be ever so severe, some men insist on it their horse will not rest so well in any stable as his own, which is against all reason. If there is good accommodation, he does an unwise thing who risks the chance of taking his horse home in preference. The best thing he can do, if the horse is distressed, is to have about two or three quarts of blood taken from him, see that he has some gruel and is properly taken care of, then go home if necessary, and send for him next day, or let the groom return by the same conveyance.

A good substitute for oatmeal is wheat flour, a pint or two of which, mixed with half a pail of warm water, can be had for sixpence at any cottage; and it would be no bad plan always to give it to your horse after a run, on his way home.

Many men breed their own horses, and ought

always to have the most perfect hunters, even before the horses have ever seen a hound, or have had a saddle on their backs, by adopting the following plan. As soon as the colt is weaned, when turned out, he has of course always a shed or stable to lie in, where he is also fed. A few yards in front of the door of the stable begin by making a slight fence, about the height of the colt's knees, which he will walk over to get to his corn. When he is quite used to this, raise the fence six inches, or more, sufficient to make him rear up, and get his forelegs over, and he will soon find it easier to jump over than draw over his hind-legs. When he does this freely, raise it still higher, till he is obliged to make a good standing leap over it every time he goes into the shed to be fed, etc. This last should be a single rail. When he is perfect at this, which he will be in the course of a month, then dig a ditch and throw up a bank with the earth, instead of the rail, or by the side of it,—which rail should be made higher to prevent his preferring it to the ditch,—and he will first walk into the ditch, then get his forelegs on the bank, and the hinder-legs on the other side of the ditch; but, in the course of a day or two, he will quietly jump on the bank. After being perfect in this, have another ditch on the other side of the bank, and he will jump on and off in a few days as well as any hunter. The writer has a thoroughbred colt at this time, only nine months old, which is as perfect at all sorts of fences as the best hunter.

The writer hopes, in selecting these extracts from a collection of his own practical observations, not to be thought too severe on any description of men who hunt with fox-hounds; for it is fair to suppose that those who have not resided in the country cannot be so much aware at times of the mischief they are doing in riding as those who are constantly resident there, and who have more opportunities of getting acquainted with the state of crops, etc. If these men would only consider this, they would not be surprised at seeing a farmer extremely irate with them for riding on a field of tares, for instance (which they had mistaken for weeds), young seeds, —that is, clover, etc., or turnips,—when there is a footpath within two yards, and this merely for the sake of keeping up a conversation by riding by the side of another man, who is riding on a path or furrow under a hedge, instead of behind him. Men being thus unconscious that they are doing mischief, makes it no matter of surprise that they flare up, or are much provoked at the coarse or rough language addressed to them by the owner of the land—a circumstance often witnessed by the writer, who has invariably proved the old proverb to be true, that " A soft word turneth away wrath "; and indeed has gone so far, at times, by way of giving a turn to the subject, as to beg those gentlemen who were threatening to horsewhip the man for his abuse, either to horsewhip him instead of the farmer, or to be patient and hear what was to be said. By this time both parties got cool, and he then commenced by stating that it was entirely through ignorance that they were doing mischief; and had the farmer only spoken civilly, these gentlemen would have instantly refrained from it, as he wished; at the same time adding, " Surely, farmer, if you are a thoroughbred Englishman, you cannot object to assist in giving these gentlemen a little amusement, who have probably been fighting the battles of your country for you!" And that he should recollect fox-hunting is not a new jumped-up sport, like steeple-chasing, but the old-established sport of the country, one cause why English officers are superior to those of almost every foreign country; that it is fox-hunting which makes them hardy, by taking them out in all weathers, and instils into them a spirit of enterprise, even beyond what they themselves had any conception of; and if the farmer is a true Briton he would be sorry to see them second (if they were military or naval men); if not officers, then, by opposition, you do all you can to prevent gentlemen from living in this country, and you would by so doing have all the large houses vacant; the consequence of which would be, you would only get half-price for your poultry and eggs and butter, independent of its keeping up the price of hay and oats. For instance, by your selling a load of hay to a gentleman for probably a greater price than the postmasters would give you, *this* is made a handle of at market; thus, on an offer being made, you say, " No, I *won't* sell for less than such a man sold for "; and so with the price of oats (which every fox-hunter should purchase of the farmers who live in the hunt, if they really do wish well to sport. It gives them an interest in the success of the pack, and they feel themselves flattered by being noticed, to which they certainly have a claim).

Any farmers hostile to fox-hunting should take the trouble of considering the benefit a pack of foxhounds is to a country, and calculate the consumption alone of corn and hay which is caused by it. Supposing, for instance, two hundred horses,—and in few countries, if any, less than that are kept, including hacks and carriage-horses, which otherwise would not be kept *there*,—they would see that, on a fair calculation, the consumption would be, for eight months only in the year, two thousand four hundred quarters of oats, at two bushels per horse per week; and if each horse have one hundredweight of hay per week for eight months, two hundred horses would consume three hundred and ninety tons of hay, etc.

It is indeed wonderful the effect of proper civility; but probably a greater proof cannot be given than this account of the following circumstance —a *fact* which actually took place in a country hunted by the writer. It happened, a year or two before he hunted the country, that a notorious character, celebrated by having ridden down the Devil's Dyke at Brighton, when riding across a field of wheat in a deep country, was accosted by the owner of the land in very rough terms. Owing to this gentleman's wearing a cap, he was mistaken for one of the whippers-in, and thus addressed: "You are a pretty sort of fellow to ride across a man's wheat in this shameful way; when the hounds be running 'tis bad enough, but to do it now is too bad; and when all the gentlemen be in the road, and you servants to behave in this way, I'll soon make you be out on't"; and actually struck the noble captain with a hedge-stake. On which he, without loss of time, made such use of his double thong, that the farmer ran away, the captain riding after him till he came to the gateway, under which there was a large drain, and into the drain the farmer got; on which the captain jumped off, hallooed, "Whoop!" and swore he had run his fox to ground; at the same time, told some person to bring the hounds to worry his fox. This so alarmed the man that he cried out for mercy; on which it was granted, and the captain left him, with the promise that he would behave better for the future. It happened, about three years afterwards, that the writer was taking his hounds across the ground belonging to this same farmer, whom he met at a gate, and was told by him that he should not ride that way across a field of newly-planted beans, which were just come up. This the writer saw, and told him that even had he not been there to warn him, he certainly should have taken the hounds, and the whole field of sportsmen round outside the field, although a considerable distance out of their way (which most assuredly he would have done at all events). Having convinced the farmer of it, he was allowed to pass, and shortly after all the others; who, by a little management by waiting, were drawn all round the field. A fox was shortly found in the cover adjoining, and after a good run was killed, when the whipper-in came up and delivered the following message from the farmer: "Sir, the farmer came up to me, just before the hounds went away with the fox, and said, 'Young man, give my respects to your master, and say, that although I am no fox-hunter —never was, nor never shall be—yet, after his behaviour to me to-day, I hope he will come here as often as he likes, and it shall not be my fault if he don't always find a fox; for I never was treated so civilly before,'" etc. The event proved his sincerity, for his cover was afterwards a sure find; and that very farmer oftener hallooed the fox away than any other man,—another proof that more flies are caught by sugar than by vinegar.

It is the duty of every man who rides hunting to take every opportunity of doing a service to the cause when he has it in his power, and that happens on many occasions which are frequently overlooked. When accidents happen to men or horses, or when a horse gets loose, men should not be slow in repaying those who assist, who, however, often get little more than a harsh word or two for being slow. A sixpence or shilling often would make the man a friend to fox-hunting, who otherwise goes home disappointed. Sometimes a man runs hard to open a gate, or to give some information, etc., for which he gets nothing—scarcely even thanks. The huntsman gets the information, but *he* has not time to throw him a trifle; and if any other person does so, the man is thankful for it, and thinks it quite correct to go to the public-house and drink success to fox-hunting, most probably in the presence of some fox-taker, who slinks away. At all events, the more friends foxes have the better; and often a civil word will gain one.

Many men who hunt are equally fond of shooting, and have friends who preserve their game, many of whom are not aware of the advantage it is to them to have a pack of fox-hounds in their covers—particularly early in the season—in cub-hunting in September and October, when they do an immense deal of good towards the preservation of pheasants and hares. By working the covers, they open the runs and tracks used by pheasants so wide that a single snare or wire, or even several, will not catch them; but before the tracks were open, every pheasant that came was sure to be caught, and equally so with the hares. The plan of catching pheasants with a single wire has not been adopted by poachers until within the last ten or twelve years, if so long; but nothing is so fatal, if set next to the oat-stubbles or fields where they feed. The writer has had ten or twelve hounds caught at a time by the foot, when cub-hunting at four or five o'clock in the morning, before the pheasants came out to feed; and he has taken several pheasants alive out of these wires, and released them. And there is no plan that can be adopted half so beneficial as to have a pack of fox-hounds to open and widen the runs in and about the covers. These wires are set as soon as it is light, and the pheasants shortly after are caught in them. The whole affair is done in a couple of hours; and it is impossible for the keeper to be everywhere during that time. Indeed, poachers have often been heard to say that a pack of fox-hounds is the greatest enemy they have.

Men who have keepers and who wish well to fox-hunting, by ordering them to set their traps for vermin in a particular way will catch all the vermin, without touching a fox; but the excuse is that traps, which are baited with rabbits, etc., as they say for small vermin, often catch foxes,— indeed more foxes than anything else. Instead therefore of baiting the trap in the usual way by placing the bait on the ground under the trap which is covered over, the proper plan, and most successful for catching small vermin, is to set the trap in a low place as before; then fasten the bait on a forked stick, about two feet long, and the other end should be stuck in the ground, leaving the bait on it about twelve inches high over the trap, when every weasel or pole-cat, etc., will come to it, and in reaching to get the bait, are certain to be caught; but if a fox comes he takes the bait without stepping on the trap, as he winds the trap and reaches over it.

Though last, not least, one hint to the fair sex, who are always ready to do a kind act to fox-hunters when they have it in their power, and many would give substantial proofs of it, if they had opportunities like the following. It happened in a country once hunted by the writer that a respectable farmer's wife had lost a great number of poultry, including some dozens of full-grown turkeys. Not far distant lived a widow lady, who heard of this loss as well as the cause of it, and, as no one could think of offering to pay the damage done to so respectable a person, a short time after the loss this lady sent a hamper of wine. It is quite unnecessary to say it, but it is a fact that no cover in that country was ever drawn without a fox, and that the lady's health was drunk at every hunt dinner with *double* honours afterwards, for it had been a standing toast previously.

N.B.—A packet of tea or tobacco, would be equally efficacious probably; not to mention a keg of brandy or hollands, which would come more properly from gentlemen who are friends to the noble sport, but have no other way of showing it.

Men who hunt are generally perfectly unacquainted with hunting terms, even the most common, and it has often been an obstacle in conversation when relating a day's sport; for even if a man has been told the meaning of any term, unless he hunts often it is not likely that he will remember it without having something to refer to, to provide which has been the object sought in compiling the following glossary.

CHAPTER IV

HUNTSMAN'S LANGUAGE EXPLAINED

Mode of Pronunciation

COVER hoick—On throwing off; for Hark into cover.
Eloo-in—Into cover.
Yoi-over—Over the fence into cover.
Edawick, Edawick, Edawick—To make hounds draw when in cover, pronounced thus for in-hoick, in-hoick, in hoick.
Yoi wind him—Ditto.
Yoi rouse him, my boys—Ditto.
Hoick Rector—A cheer to Rector, or the name of any hound which first challenged, for Hark to Rector.

Have at him old fellow—Ditto.

Hoick together, Hoick—When several hounds are heard, and are getting together.

Taa-leo—When a fox is viewed, for Tally-ho, as it can be more easily hallooed, and much louder.

Taa-leo awawoy—When a fox is seen to leave the cover, for Tally-ho away.

Gone awawoy—When a fox is gone away.

Hooi—If a person has seen a fox go away, first Taa-leo, then this halloo is used; if hounds are at a distance, it is understood that the fox has been seen.

Elope, or *Elope forward awawoy*—When some hounds are gone away, to call the rest.

Yo hote, yo hote there—When hounds are at check to make them hunt.

Forward, or *Forrid-hoick*—When some hounds have hit off the scent.

Yogueote—When hounds have gone beyond the scent, or when he wants them to come back to him; for "you go o'er it."

Yoi there, yo hote—When at check, and to make them put their noses down.

Hoick halloo—When a halloo is heard.

Yonder he goes—When in view.

Eloo at him—When the hounds are near the fox.

Eloo, eleew—When they are very close to him.

Tally-ho back—When the fox comes out, and heads back again, in preference to Taa-leo, *when used quickly.*

Eloo back—When hounds come out, to turn them back, add also, *Hark back*, and a smack of the whip.

Whoop—The death halloo.

CHAPTER V

HUNTING TERMS

A WAY—When a fox has left a cover and gone away, or the hounds are gone away.

BACK—When a fox heads back, Tally-ho back; if the hounds come out, the term is, Hark back.

BILLET—The excrement of the fox, which is known from all other by the fur of rabbits, which is nearly always to be seen in it.

BURST—The first part of a run out of cover, if quick, is called a sharp burst.

BURST HIM—A term used when a fox is killed owing to a sharp burst.

BURNING SCENT—When the hounds run almost mute owing to the goodness of the scent.

BREAST HIGH—Also a burning scent, when hounds do not stoop their heads, and go a racing pace.

CAPPING—When a fox is killed, it is the custom in some countries to cap for the huntsman; some man takes round a cap or glove, and men are expected to drop a half-crown into it. It also means, when a man takes off his hat or cap and waves it to bring on the hounds.

CARRIES—The ground after a frost adheres to the fox's feet; then the ground carries.

CARRY A GOOD HEAD—When hounds run well together owing to the scent being good, and spreading so that it extends wide enough for the whole pack to feel it; but it most frequently happens that the scent is good only on the line for one hound to get it, so that the rest not getting have nothing to lead them on, and do not get to head so as to be all abreast.

CHALLENGE—When drawing for a fox, the first hound which throws his tongue is a challenge.

CHANGED—When hounds have left their hunted fox and changed to another.

CHECK—When hounds in chase stop for want of scent, or have overrun it.

CHOP A FOX—When a fox is killed as soon as found he is said to be chopped.

CRASH—When hounds are running in cover, and it appears that every one is throwing his tongue, it is called a good crash.

CUB—A young fox, till regular hunting begins in November.

COLD-HUNTING—When hounds can scarcely feel a scent, and pick it out with difficulty.

COVER — Any wood, furze, gorse, rushes, heath, or sedge, which will hold a fox.

GOING TO COVER — Is going to the place of meeting.

CURRANT JELLY—A term used when hounds are running hare.

CHEERING—When hounds are encouraged by a halloo.

DOWN WIND—When hounds are running with the wind behind them.

DRAWING—When hounds are thrown into cover to find a fox they are drawing it.

DRAG—The scent left by footsteps of the fox on his way to his kennel that morning.

DRAIN—Underground, where foxes often run to.

DWELLING—When hounds do not get on to the huntsman's halloo; probably feeling a stale scent sometimes, till moved by the whipper-in; also, a slow huntsman is apt to dwell.

DRAFTED—When hounds are put by, not to be kept, they are drafted.

EARTHS ARE DRAWN — When a vixen fox has drawn out fresh earth, it is a proof she intends to lay up her cubs there.

EYE TO HOUNDS—A person is said to have a good eye to hounds, whose eye in the chase is always fixed on the leading hound or hounds; by which he has a great advantage over others, as he turns his horse's head immediately whichever way the leading hound does, which saves an angle.

ELOPE—A halloo, to get hounds away, and also notice for men to come away.

FLIGHTY—A hound which is not a steady hunter is called flighty; also when the scent changes from good to bad repeatedly, it is called flighty.

FORWARD—A halloo implies, to get on; or that the hounds are running ahead of you.

FEELING A SCENT—A term used when any hound smells the scent; when bad, it is said they can scarcely feel the scent.

FOIL—When a fox runs the ground over which he

has been before, it is called running his foil,—
sometimes a reason for hounds not being able
to hunt it where they have been before.

FURZE, OR GORSE—A good cover for a fox; in
some counties called gorse—in the north,
whins.

FULL CRY—When the whole pack are running
hard and throwing their tongues.

GONE TO GROUND—When a fox has got into an
earth or drain.

HARK! HALLOO!—When a person hears a halloo
at a distance, and the huntsman does not, he
should halloo, "Hark! halloo!" and point
with his whip if in sight of him.

HANDLES A PACK—A term used, speaking of a
huntsman who handles a pack well or ill.

AT HEAD—Such hounds as are going first are at
head; also such men as are first are at head.

HEADED—When a fox is going away, but is
headed; that is, turned back the way he
came.

HOLD THEM ON—For huntsmen to take the hounds
forward, and try for the scent.

HEEL.—The hounds are said to be running heel
when they get on the scent of the fox, and
run it back the way the fox came.

HIT—When hounds are at check, and recover the scent it is hitting it off. Or, the first hound that feels the scent is said to have made a good hit.

HOLD HARD — A huntsman's rate. Eager and jealous riders when they will not pull up, although pressing the hounds too closely— generally for fear that another will pass them —and so drive the hounds beyond the scent, often ruin a day's sport. Men who will not look at hounds may as well content themselves with riding steeple-chases.

HOOI—The view-halloo, if *Tally-ho* is not heard; or when hounds are at a check, and it is desirable to get them on.

HOLDING SCENT—When the scent is just good enough for hounds to hunt a fox a fair pace, but not enough to press him, though it *ought* to kill him.

KENNEL.—Where a fox lies all day in cover, to which he goes every morning before it is quite daylight, and remains in it till dark.

LINE HUNTERS are good hounds which will not go a yard beyond the scent, and keep the pack right — *invaluable* hounds; by some called plough-holders, because they hold the line.

LEFT-HANDED—Such hounds are called left-handed which are not always right, but apt to be wide, and fly without a scent. The sooner they are drafted the better, although they frequently have some excellent qualities.

LITTER, A—Young foxes, or the cubs belonging to one fox, are called a litter.

LIFTING—When hounds are scarcely able to hunt a scent across bad scenting-ground, the huntsman is induced to take them off it, and hold them forward; where he is sure to hit off the scent—probably to a halloo. This is condemned by many good sportsmen, but by others it is thought slow in a huntsman not to do it.

LYING—That part of a cover in which foxes are generally found—probably coppice wood of about two years' growth, or furze, etc.

LAID UP—When a vixen fox has had cubs, she is said to have laid up.

MAIN EARTHS—Large earths on which foxes generally breed, being difficult to get out.

METAL—When hounds are very fresh, and fly for a short distance on a wrong scent, or without one, it is called "all metal."

MOVING-SCENT—When hounds get on a scent that

is fresher than a drag, it is called a moving-scent; that is, the scent of a fox which has been disturbed by travelling.

MOBBING A FOX—Is when a fox is taken unfair advantage of, surrounded, and killed, although he had strength left to show sport if he had been allowed to go away.

MUTE—Hounds run mute when the scent is so good that the pace they go prevents their throwing tongue; but if a hound always runs mute, it is an unpardonable fault, even if in every other respect he is the best hound in the pack. The better he is, the more harm he does.

NOISY—When a hound throws his tongue without a scent, he should be drafted.

OPEN—When a hound throws his tongue he is said to open on the scent.

OPEN BITCHES—Bitches to breed from, which are not spayed, are so called.

OPEN—Earths which are not stopped are said to be open.

OWNING A SCENT—When hounds throw their tongues on the scent.

OVER IT—When hounds have gone beyond the scent in chase, it is said they are over it.

PAD—The foot of a fox.

PADDING A FOX—Is finding the print of a fox's foot.

POINT TO POINT—The distance of a run on a map by a straight line.

RACK—For a track through a fence.[1]

RABBIT EARTH, OR SPOUT—Where a fox sometimes gets into when pressed; meant to imply that it is not a regular fox-earth.

RIOT—When hounds hunt anything besides fox; the rate is "Ware riot."

SKIRTER—A hound which is generally wide of the pack. Also applied to men who are always wide of the hounds.

STROKE OF A FOX—Is when hounds are drawing. It is evident from their manner that they feel the scent of a fox, although they do not own it.

SINKING—A fox is said to be sinking when he is nearly beaten.

SINKING THE WIND—When men go down wind to hear the cry, it is called sinking the wind of the hounds.

SPAYED—Bitch hounds which are not thought good enough to breed from are spayed, probably owing to their being lathy and thin; if so, it improves them.

---

[1] The more usual term is "Meuse."—ED.

STAINED—When the ground has been passed over by cattle, or previously by the hounds.

STOOPING—When hounds will not hunt, it is said they will not stoop to the scent; that is, will not put their noses to the ground.

SLACK—When the scent is bad, hounds are apt to be indifferent, and will scarcely try to hunt their fox, and are said to be slack.

STREAMING—When hounds go over or across an open country, like a flock of pigeons, it is called streaming away.

SPEAKS—When a hound owns the scent, it is sometimes said such a hound speaks to it; if it is a safe hound it is enough to say he "speaks."

TIGHT IN HIS TONGUE—When a hound seldom throws his tongue, though not quite mute, it is said he is tight in his tongue.

TALLY-HO—The halloo when any one sees a fox, and only then. If desirable to halloo it loudly, it should be pronounced ta-a-le-o.

THROW-UP—The exact spot where the hounds lost the scent in chase is known by their throwing up their heads; and it is said they threw up here.

TICKLISH SCENT—Is when the scent varies from good to bad, and at times scarcely any in the chase, although just before it was very good.

TAILING—When hounds in chase run in a line, and not abreast, it is called tailing; generally owing to an indifferent scent.

THROW OFF—The cover into which hounds are first thrown. It is said, they threw off in that cover.

WEEDY HOUNDS—Hounds which are weakly made, and not fit to breed from.

WARE RIOT—A rate for hounds, instead of Beware riot. It is said, Ware, or Ware hare—or other riot.

WHELPS—Hound puppies, when very young.

WIND IN THEIR TEETH—When hounds are running against the wind.

YOI OVER—When a fox has crossed a ride, it is hallooed.

CHAPTER VI

FOX-HOUNDS

As well as shape, full well he knows,
To *kill* their fox, they must have nose.

IN the accompanying Plate, Fig. 1 is intended to represent a hound tolerably free from faults, in order that it may be compared with Fig. 2, which has most of the faults for which hounds are drafted, in point of shape. Few men have opportunities to compare the two in the kennel, and for them this attempt is intended. It will readily be observed that the head of No. 2 is too short and thick, with a bald face, which is generally disliked as much

Fig. 1.

T. Smith, Esq., del. Fig. 2. Facing page 232.

A GOOD HOUND AND A FAULTY ONE.

in hounds as in horses. The neck is too short and throaty, the shoulders upright and loaded; also a want of muscle in the arm and forelegs, and the most common fault in the make of hounds not being straight below the knee. No. 2 is not only crooked there, but much too long from the knee to the foot; which is also long and flat, instead of being short and round like a cat's foot. The same faults with the hinder-legs, too great length from the foot to the hock, instead of the length being from the hock upwards to the hip,—a great point in hounds and horses, and a criterion of strength for speed: for instance, compare it with a hare. No. 2. also shows weakness in the hock itself, which is small instead of large, and also a falling off in muscle in the haunches or gaskins, which should be wide and full, like a hare trussed for the spit; the loins are also weak, and would be called slack in the loins. It is also flat-sided, not deep enough in the ribs, consequently the frame is not large enough to give the lungs free play, and it could not possibly be a good-winded hound. But to judge of the frame of a hound, its head should be between the person's knees, in order that he may see the width of ribs behind the shoulders, where most hounds fall off, though this is not observed by the generality of persons who look at hounds. It is also right to stand at the side as well, to see if the legs are straight and do not stand over at the knee, or on the contrary; but standing over at the knee is often brought on by age and hard work, though frequently hounds are born so. When so, it is better not to keep them.

It is true that breeders of hounds of the present day pride themselves on having bred some as near perfection, in point of shape and make, as possible; but the question arises, when on this subject, whether such hounds will be considered perfect fifty years hence? The writer is induced to doubt this from the fact that the pictures of the best hounds—such, for instance, as were painted by the best artists of that day, Sartorius and Stubbs—are drawn with crooked legs, flat-sided, and loose in their loins, as unlike what is now thought perfection as possible; and it is fair to suppose that they were then thought handsome. Yet these hounds, which belonged to the celebrated Meynell and others, did wonders. For instance, on a trial of pace across the flat at Newmarket, they ran it in as short a time as hounds of the present day could do it, or even shorter; and, however contrary it is to the writer's principle as to the shape of hounds, he is bound to say that some few hounds are now bred *too* short, that is, too closely ribbed up to go the tremendous pace which has become the fashion in the grass countries; for it will be found, on close attention, that a lengthy hound has more freedom and goes with greater ease than one that is ribbed up and shorter. The great point therefore is to combine sufficient strength with the length, or the day will be too long also, even in the fast countries, and most assuredly so in all others—thus leaving it in doubt what will be thought perfection fifty years hence! But as to bad legs and feet, there can be no doubt that they are nearly exterminated for ever; and the only surprise is, how such legs and feet ever got into the hound at all, unless by crossing with some other sort of dog to acquire nose or courage; for, on looking at nearly all wild animals, it will be seen that their legs are straight and good. For instance, who ever saw a crooked-legged fox; their legs are straight as arrows, which is the case with most other wild animals, which never mix.

In respect to the size of fox-hounds, there is still a difference of opinion, though not so great as was the case a few years since; it being now generally considered that hounds can be too large, particularly in hilly and flinty countries. A dog of twenty-four inches is about the height to be preferred; but, notwithstanding this general opinion, the sporting world are much indebted to those gentlemen who still keep hounds of the largest size, or in the course of a few years the breed would probably dwindle below the mark, that is, if no very large hounds existed to breed from, as in all other tame animals; and however prejudiced persons may be against large hounds, or however indifferent they may be about appearances in general, still they must all agree in opinion, that a pack of fox-hounds should *look* like a pack of fox-hounds. It may be said with truth that a pack of dwarf fox-hounds, not larger than harriers, will kill as many foxes as a full-sized pack, if equal attention has been paid to the blood; but, in the present age and rage for riding, half of these small hounds would be ridden over in countries where the banks are high and ditches wide, for they cannot take them in their spring, and often fall backwards, and keep pulling each other backwards, causing much delay, and requiring more patience than men have, consequently they would be ridden over. Neither can small hounds go through deep wet land so well as a large, fair-sized hound; particularly where the water stands, as it does, in the winter, in the New Forest and other parts, which would reach up to the bodies of small hounds, and they would be swimming great part of the time.

The object of all masters and breeders of hounds is to acquire power, combined with other good qualities; but it is to be regretted that there is not more attention paid as to breeding for nose and stoutness, from which all would derive the benefit, except the wily animal. Even in the upper countries it would be more satisfactory if they oftener killed their fox, as our forest friend truly says—

> But no, with him it's all the pace;
> Then hounds will look him in the face,
> And seem to say, My noble master,
> You cannot have us go much faster;
> For we, on flying so full intent,
> A mile behind have left the scent.
>
> S. N.

This rage for pace and shape in some measure accounts for the great deficiency of nose, in comparison with what it was formerly. It is true that hounds may be, and are nearer perfection, in point of beauty. A throaty hound, for instance, is rarely seen in a pack, although very common some years back, when men thought more of hunting than of riding; but by getting rid of the throat the nose had gone with it, for a throaty hound has invariably a good nose; and that hounds were so until the end of the last century nearly all sporting pictures of hounds will prove. It happened, some years since, a gentleman purchased an old-established pack of hounds and wrote to request the writer to go and look at them before he sent away those he intended to draft. After seeing those which were to be sent away, and inquiring why they were fixed on, he was told because they were so throaty. The reply was, "As you are going to hunt a strange country, if you wish to show sport, and kill your foxes, keep those hounds, for, depend upon it, they were originally kept for their blood, not for their beauty." These hounds were kept, and during the next season the gentleman wrote to say that he had great sport, but that if he had parted with those throaty hounds, he should not have killed one fox in ten that he had done, for they were the only hounds that could hunt a cold scent. Of course the plan is to breed for both beauty and goodness; and it is much to be regretted that a cross so seldom nicks, as one could wish, without faults of generations back coming out, one side or the other—probably not half a dozen times in a man's lifetime—owing to the age of the hound being past before it can be well known enough to repeat it; for even if it nicks the first time, the produce will be three years old before they can be depended on; even if they then show their qualities, the sire must be five or six years old, as he must have been most likely three when the bitch was put to him, as no man likes to breed from an untried dog in general, particularly with a valuable bitch. In addition to this difficulty of repeating the cross when it nicks, it is ten to one but that some accident happens to either one or the other; no sort of difficulties should prevent the repetition whilst it is possible,—that is, if the dog and bitch are in any part of the kingdom.

If a man is determined in breeding to attend to nose and stoutness, he will be sure to succeed in getting a good pack, and one which will go faster, take the season through, than those men who bred for beauty and pace; and he need not fear of also getting a pack clever in shape too.

The writer has made many experiments in the breeding of fox-hounds; and, in consequence of the circumstance that most clever men who have distinguished themselves have been the offspring of clever mothers, the following plan was tried, more than once, in order to discover whether young hounds inherit most good qualities from the dog or from the bitch. Having selected a bitch of three seasons, which had never distinguished herself, either as good in drawing, in the chase, or in cold-hunting, although having no decided fault as to slackness, and put this bitch to some dog which was considered to have most of the good qualities required in a fox-hound, the produce inherited only some of them.

He also tried the experiment the other way, selecting a dog hound of three or four seasons, which had not shown himself a good drawer, good in the chase, or a good cold-hunter. This dog was put to an extraordinary good bitch, which had most of the qualities required; and the produce was in every instance superior. It is fair to add, that the last-mentioned bitches were from the best blood, which will generally prove to be the case, if they are remarkable, although probably a generation or two back.

It is a remarkable fact in breeding, and worthy of notice, that if a young hound has any peculiarity which the sire had, such as standing in a particular way in the kennel, or in following closely the huntsman's horse, or any other trick of the sire, he will also generally inherit with it all his good qualities, and may be bred from without fear the first year; and if this (which is the only way of finding out a cross which nicks early) is a lucky one, it will be known soon enough to be repeated several times. But it must not be till after the produce with that bitch has been tried; consequently two years after it will be known, and the same bitch can be put to him again, but not till then.

The writer was once asked the following question in the company of four masters of hounds, We four agree in thinking that bitches are quicker in cover than dogs; what say you? Yes; not because they are bitches, but because they are smaller, and can go with greater ease after a fox in thick cover, brambles, furze, etc., than dogs; but find dogs the same size as the bitches, and hunt them together, and they will be as often first as the bitches; and much oftener right, not being naturally so flighty. It might have been added, that to have hounds perfect for work in every sort of country, the dogs should look like bitches, and the bitches should look like dogs.

It may appear paradoxical, but it is nevertheless true, that the proof of a hound's goodness is, that he is never remarkable during a run; and there are many good sportsmen who would prefer a hound of this nature than one which is oftener seen at head than any of the rest. Of course a hound that is not remarkable is never last, or where he should not be, but holds the line, and is what is called by some a good line-hunter, which is the criterion of all goodness; that is, if he hunts and *drives* a scent, too, without dwelling on it.

It is observable that large young hounds are not so much disposed for riot as small ones, when they are entered; and one reason is that they cannot follow it where a small one can, which is frequently proved by a brother and sister. And when large dog hounds do not work a fox in thick brambles like the bitches, it is that the bitches stick to their fox and can follow him without difficulty, when a large dog hound passes the small run or track where the fox went under brambles or bushes, and goes round, which the fox soon finds out and does not leave it so soon as when the bitches press him closely by their following him, for they can

> Every inch his footsteps trace.

It admits of a doubt, whether hunting dogs and bitches separately is an advantage, or whether anything is gained by it, except appearance, as it makes the packs more even. It is true that the bitches are quicker as a pack than dogs, but they do not always show the most sport, or kill the most foxes. They are apt to be flighty, and unless very strong, with four- and five-year hunters, they will not kill anything like so many as the dogs, and in a woodland country it is decidedly objectionable. They are not so free with their tongues, and often slip away without any one knowing it; on this account alone it is desirable to have some dog hounds, which will also assist in holding the line for them. And if a complaint is made that the dog hounds have not quite dash enough, let a few flying bitches go with the dogs, and it will improve both packs.

The plan of spaying young bitches which are light and weedy, answers beyond the belief of those who have not tried it; so much so, that although when spayed they were too light to breed from, in the course of a year or two they furnish so much as to make it often a cause of regret that they cannot be bred from; but it ought not to cause regret, as there is little doubt that the improvement is owing to the operation. It is well known that it also improves the nose, and they often become the best cold-hunters in the pack, although very different before, and far better than the sisters which were not spayed; besides which, they hunt generally several years longer than open bitches. It is no uncommon thing to see a spayed bitch leading the pack after hunting seven or eight seasons. The cheapest pack of fox-hounds to keep is a pack of spayed bitches; they do more work with less food than any others, and always look in good condition; but unluckily this cannot be adopted generally, on account of futurity. One great objection to bitches hunting alone is that there is not so much music; and it will be noticed that if a few dog hounds hunt with a pack of bitches, even they will not throw their tongues so freely after a short time: evil communications, they say, corrupt good manners; unless it is thought that the bitches do not give them so much time to talk about it. This may be the case, but unless they can say they have killed their fox when they go home, they had better have had a little more chat together.

There is a prejudice against cutting dog hounds which are slight and weedy, but it improves their appearance as much as it does the bitches; and it also improves their nose, and their power for work, and in every other respect, as in the other case. It is a good plan if a dog hound is quarrelsome in the kennel, if it is not desirable to preserve the sort,— which should be well considered first, or the improvement in the hound afterwards may be the cause of constant regret. But there are always stallion hounds to be found equally good.

There are certain faults which should never be overlooked, let the hound be ever so good in every other way. A mute hound is unpardonable; if he should be in every other respect perfect, so much the greater reason for drafting him. He finds your fox in cover, and goes on with him; the rest of the pack get together on this line, presently come to a check, then get away and another check. You see a man at work, and ask, "Have you seen a fox?" "No; but I seed a whitish hound go along as fast as he could go just now." This is our mute friend who goes away without saying a word; the consequence is that his having passed along the line of scent, although the leading hounds can hunt it, and do a certain distance, yet at times they find the hound's scent as well, and do not much like it. Eventually, nine times out of ten, it brings them to a check every five hundred yards; and, if it is a bad scent, much oftener. As an old sportsman in the New Forest once said to the writer, who had remarked to him on a hound having been first all day: "I'll tell you how it is; d—n him, he runs mute."

You set two men to run up a hill, one of them to halloo all the way up and the other to run mute, and you will find that the man who ran mute will get to the top before the other gets half way. Indeed, when hounds go the best pace, they *must* go mute; and the few that do throw their tongues are those whimpering behind, because they cannot get up.

Another fault is skirting. This is also often a source of regret, for many capital hounds become skirters, and it is often a proof of their having greater sagacity than the rest. How very frequently do you see the skirting hound make the most beautiful casts and surprising hits of his own accord. But one skirter makes many, both of hounds and men; and creates the greatest confusion should he get on another fox, etc. In short, there is no end to the mischief he creates. You see him slipping down a ride to cross the line of the fox, before the pack, and bring them to a check; or crossing the line of another fox, etc.

Notwithstanding this, a pack of skirters would be as likely to kill their fox the first year, if not more so, than any other; and it may be often remarked that a new pack kill more foxes the first year than any other year afterwards,—which pack consist principally of draft hounds; consequently, many are skirters, probably half the pack; but as they are strangers to the country, they do not skirt so much, but hold together better; and always being at work as they are (in their own way), against so many heads a fox has not much chance. The success may also be in some measure partly attributed to a new pack not entering many young hounds the first year.

Hounds that dwell too much on the scent, or that throw their tongues when behind the pack in chase, should also be drafted.

Bitches are generally more unsteady than dogs; but if either are not broken from it the first year, they seldom become perfectly steady afterwards.

The sooner bitches are put to dogs after the first of January the better, as few packs are strong enough to spare many bitches early in the season; and when they do, they generally feel the difference, that is, if the bitches are worth breeding from; therefore it is much better to have a greater number of bitches than usual, than to weaken the pack by taking out the brood bitches, as no doubt the earlier the whelps come the better. The bitches had better not hunt for a week after taking the dog, nor be hunted longer than a month after that time, making five weeks after. The most favourite blood should be sent to the best walks, butchers, etc., as, according to an old saying, "All beauty goes in at the mouth."

As before stated, the two great points to attend to in breeding are stoutness and nose; therefore it is best only to breed those that are stout as wire and that never get slack, and those which can hunt a cold scent. The two qualities often go together; for it is the stoutness which makes a hound willing to try to hunt and make use of his nose, which a slack hound would not try to do. But much of this depends on the huntsman. If he is persevering, his pack will soon become hunters; but they must be *born* with good noses, and none ought to be allowed to be bred from which have not.

Every huntsman, at times, must feel disposed to say that he will not breed from any hound that will not always draw well; and, doubtless, he would adopt a most sensible plan, for almost all hounds that draw well are stout, and have good noses to feel a drag, as they must do in drawing; and if some hounds draw well in the afternoon (when the great part of the pack are slack and will not draw), it is because they are stout.

The sagacity of old fox-hounds is far beyond that

known of most animals, and in nothing greater probably than in their finding their way home great distances. The writer was once left upwards of forty miles from his kennel, after an extraordinary run, which was described by Nimrod some years back, and two hounds were missing which were seen to go off with another scent at the end of the run, when a fresh fox crossed them. Nothing was heard of them for three days; but on the fourth they both found their way to the kennel, not looking the worse for their travels. Had they followed the track of the hounds that night, or even next morning, it would not have been extraordinary, of course.

The following is another proof of sagacity. Not long since the writer went to see a celebrated pack throw off, he being mounted on a hack. When they were running hard, and going across the open —having left a large cover behind them—at the edge of which he pulled up, on seeing them at a check more than a quarter of a mile off, when they came to a road. Just at this time the whipper-in rode up to him and asked where they were. On their being pointed out to him, it was suggested by the writer that he had better wait a few minutes and see what was to happen, as the huntsman was properly making his cast forward, after the pack had been held on by the side of the road for some distance, and no touch of a scent. At this time a couple and a half of old hounds were seen cantering back, lashing their sterns on the very line they had gone forward, and were coming straight to the cover, occasionally turning round to listen if the pack was running. When at length they got nearly to where the whipper-in and writer were, that is, close to the large wood, he was in the act of smacking his whip and rating them on, when the writer requested him to be quiet and see the result, which was that, as soon as they got back to the cover-side, they hit off the scent, the fox having come back the line he went. On which the whip held up his cap, gave a view-halloo, and brought the pack back; after which the fox made the same point over a fine country and was killed. But the cause of the fox heading back was a waggon and horses, which the writer could see up the road, but which the huntsman was not aware of; and it must have been exactly opposite the spot where the fox would otherwise have crossed the road, at the time he got there, and headed back.

CHAPTER VII

THE FOX

IT is scarcely possible to describe, either with the pencil or the pen, the beauty and powers of this extraordinary animal; it has often been tried on canvas with as little success as with the pen. If an artist was desired to paint the most perfect animal in the shape of a quadruped, it would be not *a* fox, but *the* fox, for they are all so nearly alike in point of symmetry; and, on examination, it will be found that no animal has so much muscle in proportion to its size, and the bone, like that of a thorough-bred horse, is like ivory: in point of strength of loins, nothing can exceed it. It is only necessary to notice the width of frame behind the shoulders, which gives so much space for the lungs, and which accounts for the extraordinary wind it has often shown itself to possess, to the no small surprise and disappointment of both hounds and men; for there are foxes which, if they have time to prepare themselves for work, will defy any pack to kill, even with a good scent, and they will have enough to do even with a burning scent, without having the usual accidents of checks, etc., in a run. These are seasoned foxes which one meets with now and then—for a very good reason, that they are always awake; and either steal away, or leave hounds too far behind to allow of a familiar acquaintance.

The illustration represents the finish of a good run with the writer's hounds in the Hambledon country, 1828. The fox ran into a chalk-pit with the hounds close at him, and a hound was seen by the writer and many others hanging to the fox by his brush for several minutes, till the fox was exhausted and fell amongst the hounds below.

The fox is the most deceiving animal as to powers. Many huntsmen have gone out determined, if there is a good scent, to kill their fox in a short time, with the same feeling that many went

T. Smith, Esq., del.   Facing page 252.
FINISH TO A GOOD RUN WITH THE HAMBLEDON HOUNDS, 1828.

A FRESH FOX.

T. Smith, Esq., del.

A BEATEN FOX.

Facing page 253.

out to *the* Carlos[1] in Spain, but have found out that he takes more killing than they bargained for, being a much stouter fellow than was expected, and the only chance was a sharp brush at first.

The two sketches of a fox are intended to represent one that is quite fresh, and one that is rather beaten. Few men have opportunities to observe the difference, and consequently mistake a fresh fox for a hunted one, and often declare most positively that the fox they have seen is the hunted one; and the huntsman is induced to go away with him, but finds, to his regret, that it is a fresh one, when all the horses are dead beaten, as well as the fox which is left behind. If this hint should be the means of making men more cautious how they give so decided an opinion, it will be a point gained. It is worthy of notice, when a fox is beaten he goes very high, with his back up, etc.

It may be that some of these observations on this animal are not generally known, but they have been ascertained by experience to be correct. In the first place, that a fox breeds but one litter of cubs in a year, and that all the vixens in the country lay up their young about the same time, that is, within six weeks, or thereabouts, making the 25th

[1] Charley, a slang term for a fox; origin, Charles Fox.

of March about the middle of the breeding season. Old men and sportsmen who have paid the greatest attention to the habits of the fox appear to agree on that point. One solitary instance has come to the knowledge of the writer during his life which has been much devoted to these subjects generally, and that was most remarkable. It was related to him by the Hon. William Gage, who actually saw a litter of young foxes, about one month old, in the month of February 1832, in one of his covers in Hampshire. Fortunately for the pleasure of fox-hunting, this is a solitary exception, but of which there can be no doubt, as they were brought in by the keeper, and were often seen afterwards. It is no less certain, that it is an almost unheard-of circumstance for a fox to breed earlier than about the general time mentioned above; otherwise instances must have occurred to disprove this assertion. The cubs would be discovered in some way, either by accident or when digging out a fox; or keepers and earth-stoppers would see that the earths were used by cubs. Nothing of the sort ever occurs until the beginning of the month of March, when the earths are drawn by the vixens; and about the end of the month and in April, cubs are frequently found above ground in the New Forest. Several instances have occurred when the vixen fox has been seen to steal away from a furze cover, carrying a cub in her mouth, when she has heard the hounds drawing; and nothing is more common than for a vixen to remove her cubs, when they have been disturbed, or the place visited by any one. They have been known to carry away a whole litter two or three miles in one night, when the cubs were about ten days old, about which age they begin to see.

The food of foxes, as is well known, varies in different countries, except in rabbits, which they always will get if they can, as they prefer them to any other description of food; and the proof of it is that a bet of a hundred to one can be had that every billet of a fox has rabbits' fur in it. That they do prefer rabbits is easily proved to be the case, by confining in some place a fox, and with him a rabbit and every other sort of food, live or dead, that can be thought of, and he will take the rabbit first to a certainty. This is not *a* great reason, but *the* great reason why keepers dislike foxes; for every fox destroys rabbits in one year sufficient to have supplied the keeper with gin; consequently, when he sees a fox, he loses his spirits as well as his temper. The fox finds the rabbits in the stops when very young, and when they are not to be had he lives upon the old ones, both of which are often the keeper's perquisites. This is so well known, that many gentlemen who wish well to hunting will not allow their keepers to sell the rabbits. In the New Forest and elsewhere foxes live principally on beetles, the wings of which are seen in their billets; if near the sea they live a great deal on fish which they find on the shore. It is not here pretended to assert that foxes will never do any mischief, but that, just as when once a dog takes to killing sheep, he continues to do so; so with a fox, if one learns to take poultry he continues to do so till taken himself. But there are hundreds of old foxes which never tasted a fowl; nor do they commit a twentieth part of the mischief to game that is sometimes talked of by keepers, who tell their masters that it is no use to preserve pheasants whilst there are foxes. Surely some signs would be left in covers, if foxes did destroy so many pheasants,—they would not eat up feathers and all; and the writer can, with a safe conscience, declare that he never saw three places where a pheasant had been destroyed by a fox during the whole time he hunted hounds, although constantly looking whenever he went in covers abounding with pheasants and foxes at the same time.

The following is a system which has been known to be adopted by keepers who are determined enemies to foxes, and who wish their masters to believe, not only that they are very attentive to their duty, but that foxes do much more harm than they really do, as *they* say (it being the time they have cubs). The keeper adopts this plan: he shoots a hen pheasant, and having cut it into several pieces he lays the feathers, which are bloody, about the cover, probably in twenty different places. Shortly afterwards he begs his master to go and see the damage the fox has done, and takes him round to all the places where the feathers, etc., are, and persuades his master that there has been a hen pheasant killed at each place. This trick is played at other seasons as well; by which means, having apparently shown such a convincing proof, he often gains permission to kill the fox,—"*Only in a quiet way*, you know, sir!"

There are other charges against foxes which they do not deserve. One is that of taking away lambs from a sheepfold. The writer does not mean to say that such a thing has never happened, —though it has never been proved to him,—but the following did happen. A respectable farmer, who used to hunt regularly with his hounds (and who will probably see this), told him that he was sorry to say there *was* a rogue that had taken away a lamb several nights following, and begged that the hounds might draw the hedgerows about, and find this villainous fox. A few days afterwards he came and urged it more, saying that other lambs had been taken. As it was an unlikely country to find, a by-day was fixed on. Every hedge and hedgerow at all likely was drawn without the slightest appearance of a fox having been there. The hounds were then trotted off to the next wood, about a mile, shortly found, and after a good run killed their fox. The brush was given to the farmer, who went home well satisfied that this was the right fox, and told his shepherd of it, who was equally pleased. A few days afterwards the farmer came again, and said, that having lost some more lambs since the hounds were there, his shepherd, unknown to him, had set a trap for the fox, and in it next morning was found, not a *fox*, but his master's favourite pointer, which he at once destroyed, and never lost another lamb.

The likely part of a cover to find a fox in is where it is low enough to admit the rays of the sun to reach him in his kennel during some part of the day if possible, to which he returns as soon as daylight appears, and is seldom seen after dusk in the morning, unless he is disturbed or in quest of a vixen in the month of February; but cubs are apt to move in the daytime when they are nearly half-grown, until they have been hunted or frightened. Foxes, in some countries where there are forests with old trees, or pollards covered with ivy, are often known to be found lying in them, having made their kennel a considerable height from the ground, in proof of which the following fact happened to the writer, when he had just killed a fox, although after a good run, in Savernake forest. The keeper came up and said, "Sir, here is another ready for you up in an oak-tree!" The novelty of the thing induced him against his better judgment to see the result of turning him off his roost. The hounds were taken aside some distance, and a man climbed up the tree; but the fox, which could be seen, did not move till the man shook the ivy on which he lay, when off he jumped, and had not the under branches saved him he must have been killed. As it was, he rebounded on reaching the ground, three feet at least, and away he went, none the worse for his flight. The hounds were shortly lain on, and went straight to some immense woods; and the day finished with running three or four foxes at dark. In Sherwood Forest, Nottinghamshire, and in other forests, foxes often lie in hollow trees, and very frequently run into them and save themselves when hunted; but sometimes are bolted by terriers, which has been made a subject for pictures in those countries.

When a litter of cubs is known of, the sooner they are moved the better; if in an earth, apply a match of brimstone, made thus—melt the brimstone over a fire, then spread on a sheet of brown paper; cut it in strips, an inch or two wide, then split the end of a stick about eighteen inches long, put in one of the strips, and stick the other end into the ground and set fire to it; or smear the side of the hole with gas-tar—much the shortest way—and the old one will take the cubs away where they probably may not be found again. This should be done when cubs are *very* young, or fox-takers will have them if they are old enough to take care of themselves, or even to eat. They have dogs which can go into the main earths, and are taught to bring the cubs out alive in their mouths; therefore when they are moved these fox-takers will not readily find them, and must be seen if they are looking about for them; and at this time of the year it is well worth while to employ some persons to look out for these customers.

Cubs which are bought and turned out seldom come to anything, although they are as fine-looking foxes as wild ones, unless they are allowed to remain where they are put down till late in the season, at all events till after Christmas, by which time they have learnt to find their own food, and have probably been moved by shooters, dogs, etc., and have learnt their way about from cover to cover. But if a litter of cubs has been put down in a wood and regularly fed, although they are all fine foxes, and hunted so early as September, in October or November they may be found once; but they will be frightened away from the ground they know and from their food to a strange country, where they will be in a starving state, which will oblige them to visit dangerous places, sheepfolds, etc., and they will nearly all, most probably, be killed by shepherds' dogs or others; not one may ever find its way back. This is a caution well worthy of attention by those who happen to have foxes brought them which were bred in their own country; but it is strange that any one will buy his neighbour's foxes, for how would any man like to hear of a neighbour buying his pheasants' eggs? for on both sport equally depends.

The difference in the sagacity of young foxes bred up in the above manner, and those bred up naturally by the vixen, at the same age, is almost beyond belief, owing, of course, to their education by the old vixen. One proof amongst many known the writer gives. After killing a cub with his hounds, another ran into a rabbit hole; the whipper-in got hold of the brush, and in pulling the cub out, he pulled off half the brush. The hounds were gone home, but he brought home this cub, about eight miles from the cover; and in the same evening it was marked and turned out close by the kennel. Nothing more was thought about it till near Christmas, when the same wood was drawn where this fox was bred and dug out. He was again found, and after a good run was killed; and he was known by his short brush, and the mark. This young fox, in the month of October, had found his way back to this cover, having had to cross *two wide* rivers, and travel eight miles.

Therefore, when young foxes are brought, it is by far the best plan, if possible, to find out exactly where they came from; to do which, the whipper-in should go back with the man who brought them, on the pretence of wishing to see if there are any more, or some other reason, and ascertain exactly where they were taken from; then, unknown to the man, go if possible the same night at dark and put the cubs down again in some place, with a little food, where they cannot get away of themselves; and although they may have been taken some days, the vixen will be sure to be looking for them, and will find them out, and take care of them; which, by going very early next morning, he will find is the case, and ten to one but they are safe. The only use of cubs which are turned down is to blood the young hounds, and save thereby the necessity of killing your native cubs.

Foreign foxes, it is said, will not show such sport as the foxes of the country; this may, or may not be, for the fact of having had an extraordinary run with a decided French fox induces the writer to have a better opinion of them. This was a two years old fox which, through not having been moved the first year he was turned down, survived, and was as stout as any English fox. But it is all waste, both of money and trouble, unless they are left quiet for some time, as stated above, till they get seasoned. That such was the case with this Frenchman, the following account will prove. He was found by the writer in the outskirts of his country, and ran directly straight away through the adjoining hunt, and was killed twelve miles from where he was found. It was remarked that the hair on the brush was longer and lighter coloured than usual, and the fur on the skin was finer and softer; a member of the hunt in which it was killed took up the fox, before he was given to the hounds, and exclaimed at once, "D—d odd!" and it was ascertained by a mark to be one of a lot from France the year before.

It is probable that some may think it injudicious to make known that such things are ever imported into this country, but these persons should also bear in mind that it may have quite a contrary effect, for when men who are hostile to fox-hunting think that they can destroy the means of sport, they ought to know that any man who likes to be at the expense of it, can import a thousand foxes in a month.

The writer takes the opportunity of declaiming against turning down foxes, having been fortunate in hunting a country so well stocked as not to require it; but if it were necessary to resort to any method, he would most assuredly adopt the following, which is the only good and sure plan of getting foxes in parts of a country where there are no holding covers, and in which part of the country it may be desirable to some residents, all of whom, if they have any land, have it in their power, at a trifling expense, to get native foxes; and the greater the distance from large covers, the better will be the runs, if these foxes get to them. It often happens that a vixen fox, with or without cubs, is dug out, and brought to the master of the hounds, probably by accident, or from a part of the country which is seldom or never hunted. When this is the case, the plan is to make a false earth,— a drain about three feet deep or more, where necessary, about twelve inches wide; to be firmly covered over with thick boards, or rough timber; then cover it with earth, well rammed down; the drain to be about ten yards long, at the end a space about three feet square. Then get a light, but strong chain, and a strong collar, and chain up the vixen; the end of the chain to be fastened about six feet within the hole, so that when the fox goes in to the end, she draws into the drain all the chain. The cubs to be put in with her. They will remain with the vixen until they have found their way about the country; and by Christmas they will have found out the nearest covers, and will soon after take to them. But the vixen is to be still kept chained up as long as she lives, and she will breed a litter of cubs every year, for the dog foxes will be sure to find her out. The situation most desirable would be near a pond or stream of water, when it would not be necessary for any person to carry a supply of water, and it should be in some open place, within sight of a cottage where the person who takes care of her lives. A butcher should be engaged to supply some sheeps' paunches, or offal of some sort, twice a week ; this, and the remains of poultry, etc., from the great houses near, will be food for her. The advantages of this plan over that of turning down and feeding cubs without a vixen, is that, when these cubs are found or frightened after they take to the woods, they will come straight to the vixen where they were bred, and be safe until they are old enough to show sport, when the earth could be stopped by an iron grating the day the hounds were expected. Not so with those turned down and fed by hand, if they are hunted before Christmas, or before they have learnt the country and how to find their own food. On being driven away from what has been their home, they know not where they are, or their way back, and are seldom heard of or seen again; at least such is known to be the case with those that have been marked.

It may possibly be suggested that it would be easy for some person to come in the night and take away this vixen fox. This is a mistake, for she would draw into the earth the whole chain, six feet within the opening of the drain or earth, when any person approached her; and it would be necessary for them to dig her out, which would be no easy task. But it should be recollected that a fox in this state is not a wild animal, and a person would be just as liable to be prosecuted for stealing it, as he would be for breaking open a stable and stealing a horse; or how does it happen that tame foxes which are chained up in yards, etc., are never stolen in preference to a dog? One is a sure sale, the other not.

One of the great objections against turning down foxes is that they are generally infected with mange, most particularly those purchased of regular fox-sellers, or, more properly, of those receivers of stolen goods, for such they are. This, when easily and satisfactorily explained, will probably be the means of deterring some masters of hounds from encouraging so nefarious, unhandsome, and dishonourable a practice, that is, supposing these foxes were bred in any hunting country; for the consequence of it is that the mangy young foxes, in the course of a short time, find out all the fox-earths near, and instinctively make use of them, thereby infecting them with mange, so that every native which enters these earths for some time afterwards, catches the disease. The reason why foxes, purchased as above described, become thus mangy is, that this atrocious trade is generally kept by men who reside in London, and they have not a room sufficiently large to keep them clean; and when once that one room has been infected, it is scarcely possible to cleanse it. There is another cause to which the introduction of mangy foxes into the country may be attributed, that is, owing to a fox having by some means taken poisoned food, but not sufficient to destroy him. This is well known to have that effect on all animals, and in none more than a fox and a rat, both of which in the course of time recover their health; but it is at least two years before they recover their coats or fur. That they do recover is certain, although it has not been discovered what its instinct has applied as a cure; but to something there is little doubt, as we may judge by the canine race, for unless a dog which is affected by mange is not properly attended to, he will scratch himself to death, or become unfit to live, if fastened up and not at liberty to use his own remedy. The proof that foxes do recover their health and strength after losing all their hair or fur, is the fact of their showing extraordinary sport with hounds; indeed some of the best runs on record are with mangy foxes. One of the best the writer ever had with his own hounds was from a patch of gorse on Ilsley Downs. The fox went away almost in sight of the hounds, and continued in sight of the men for several miles over the downs, a racing pace, and was killed after forty minutes almost without a check, when it was found he had scarcely a hair on his body, and not one on his brush, or rather what should have been his brush. This run will not be forgotten by many Oxonians. The writer had seen during the run that the fox was mangy, and when in a wood, and getting near a large breeding earth, he rode wide of the hounds, and got on the earth just in time to prevent the fox going in, and in consequence she was killed within fifty yards of it; and, although it was a vixen, it was not a source of regret, though so late in the season that the earths were opened. It would have been no mercy to have saved her, for if she had lived to breed a litter of cubs, every one of them would have been affected with the mange, and they would have infected others. To have mangy foxes in a country must be considered a great nuisance, and one way of reducing the chances of getting them is by destroying the earths, or, at all events, stopping them up during the hunting season, according to the plan hereafter described (*vide* Earth-stopping).

The usual or rather the greatest age of foxes in general does not appear to be very well known. But that they live to the age of ten or twelve years the writer has proved, by having hunted and killed a fox with a short brush, which was called the stump-tailed fox, and had been known and hunted eight or nine years before he went into the country, and which when killed had scarcely a tooth left, indeed nothing but the stumps.

Foxes are thought to run stoutest about the middle of the winter,—from the beginning of December to the end of January. And from the circumstance that the fur of all animals is most valuable in the midst of winter, it is fair to suppose that they are stronger and in better condition at that time, consequently more fit for work. But after that time, in the month of February, the dog foxes are much easier killed than in any other month, owing to their travels at night after the vixens, which travels continue till the month of March, when it is still no uncommon thing to find two or three dog foxes in the same wood; but though such is the case with dog foxes, the vixens often run very stoutly in February. Owing to the above circumstance there is greater difficulty in finding foxes during that month than any other, as they congregate in the neighbourhood of some vixen, near where a litter of foxes is usually bred; and, consequently, that is the only part likely to be a tolerably sure find at this particular time of the year.

It has been asserted in a sporting publication, not long since, as well as on other occasions, that if a fox when he is moved by hounds is not pressed in the chase, he will only keep a certain distance before the pack. According to that idea, it matters not what pace the hounds go; as the fox stops when hounds come to a check. But this assertion is not borne out by the facts, at all events only occasionally, where a fox has been often disturbed by the hare-hounds, or other dogs; on which occasions he will not go straight away, or keep on. But that good wild foxes do not dwell in the way asserted above, innumerable proofs can be given of the following description. On one occasion a fox was found by the hounds belonging to the writer in an outside cover which adjoined an open country for ten or twelve miles, and after a ring or two was killed in about an hour. A gentleman who came late to cover, met a fox two miles off, going straight across the open above described, of which he spoke; and, consequently, it was decided that the hounds should meet there, in three weeks' time, with the hope of finding this gallant fellow. The hounds met and drew the same cover for him, and very soon two foxes were on foot. After running hard in cover for half an hour, the whipper-in, who was placed where he could see if any fox took that open country, rode up and said he was gone away. The hounds were with difficulty stopped from the fox, which remained in cover, and clapped on the flyer—but with a coldish scent, owing to the start he got; nothwithstanding which, they went straight as possible across the open for nearly twelve miles, quite out of sight of any cover, or scarcely a fence to hide a fox, and then came to a fatal check, owing to a flock of sheep having gone along a road just before the hounds, etc. When they were turned towards home, a shepherd came up and said he saw the same fox that day three weeks come over the open downs—exactly the same line the hounds came that day, and about the same hour; and no doubt this was the same fox which was seen that day, which is sufficient to prove that good foxes at all events do go on, whether hounds are after them or not. And probably this may do away the wonder and surprise that some men express, namely, how strange it is that foxes can beat hounds which are kept in such high condition, and in such constant wind; for there is little doubt but that most good foxes in a country which is hunted regularly, move whenever they hear a pack of hounds in chase run through or near the cover in which they lie, and go straight away in another direction. As such is known to be the case now and then, of course it oftener happens when it is *not* known; for nothing is more common than for a master of hounds, or a man who hunts, to be told by some person the next day, that he met or saw a fox several miles off, going like a hunted one in an opposite direction to where the hounds had run about the same time the day before. But much of this depends on the sort of covers in a country; for a fox will lie much longer and quieter in a furze or gorse cover than in any other, for more reasons than one that the writer can give. It is pretty sure that a hunted fox will

T

not pass through it, although he often does through other sorts of covers, which do not impede him; consequently, a fox lying in a wood and hearing hounds running through it, or near it, will be off: therefore they have more exercise than many are aware of. Independent of this, foxes get regularly every night sufficient to keep them in wind; and some even in better than hounds, which are old foxes that have been hunted, and are too cunning to over-fill themselves with food, although it does sometimes happen, probably by picking up a wounded bird, or something just before they go to their kennel for the day. But these are accidental circumstances; and when in such a state, foxes are shortly killed, although the day before it would have taken the same pack four hours to kill, even if they did at all, and with a good scent; for, as before asserted, there are foxes which, when fit to go, can beat any hounds; and that these foxes are not known, is to be accounted for by their stealing away, and hounds not being on terms do not know much about them as to their stoutness.

Many foxes are also often abused, and pronounced great brutes, etc., and that the sooner they are killed the better, in order that they may go and find a good one, merely because the fox hangs

Sufficient work for the next week.

in cover, and runs rings in it for half an hour or more. This is no proof of his being a bad one, but often the reverse; for by this time the ground gets stained where the hounds have been over it once or twice, and the pack do not continue to press him as at first, and he gets time to lighten himself; and then, being fit to go, he takes the open country and rarely is beaten, but has given those gentlemen's horses sufficient work for the next week, who abused him in the morning. Neither is it a proof of a fox being a bad one, his going to ground shortly after being found. It is the greatest proof of his sagacity, especially on a good scenting day. This is acquired by age and experience, which the following account with the writer's hounds may prove. The meeting was near a fashionable town, and it being the day after a gay fancy ball in that part, a large field were present, when to the delight of all a fox was found, which, after a ring or two in the adjoining covers with a capital scent, went to a by-earth, to the great annoyance of every one, more particularly of the writer; and no small share of rating got the earth-stopper, who declared that he had put to, that is, merely thrust some sticks into it, which was not a regular earth. The hounds laid at it, and were baying, although there was only a possibility for a fox to have drawn himself in, probably owing to their hounds lying and scratching at the earth. But thinking it possible the fox was not gone in, he trotted off with the hounds to the farther end of the small cover, when the hounds hit off the scent; and the fox having got a little law, went down wind nearly as straight as possible by the map sixteen miles, when the hounds ran into him, just after crossing a wide piece of water, which did the business for him. So good a run was it, that one or two of those who saw the finish will recollect the following exclamation, when the fox was in hand: "Now, I don't care if I never kill another fox!"—and yet this one would, it appeared, have gone to ground in five minutes after being found, if he could. The foregoing anecdote not only proves that the best foxes do go to ground early, but also that it is more than probable that many of the best foxes generally lie under ground, when there are large earths. The remedy for which will be proposed hereafter (*vide* Earth-stopping). It will probably be noticed that in the above run the scent was good—which of course a fox must be aware of, as he lives by hunting—and this was probably the cause of his trying to go to ground.

There is little doubt that on many days when hounds cannot find, and on which days the scent has been proved to be capital, foxes are under ground; they are not afraid to stay above ground in bad scenting weather, but take care to be out of the way in good. And on those days, if a pack of hounds come suddenly upon him—that is, to draw the cover where he is lying, before he has an opportunity to steal off—it will often be observed that he will lie till they almost tread on him, if late in the day and no drag; which is one proof that the scent does not come from the body or breath of the animal, but from the touch. And by his lying quiet in his kennel, the scent does not exude from under him, that is, from the ground he lies upon, until he moves away, according to the old song—

> And Saucebox roars out in his kennel.

But the most convincing and satisfactory proof, that the scent does come from the touch of the animal is that, when the ground carries after a frost, there is even a burning scent on turf and sound hard ground, until the hounds get on a fallow or ploughed ground, when they will feel the scent for a few paces only, and it will entirely go until they are held across the ploughed field; and when they are again on turf or sound ground, or going through the fence, they will hit off the scent immediately, as the foot is clean and touches the ground; which is accounted for by the foxes' feet gathering earth as soon as they tread on the ploughed ground, which on being pressed adheres to the bottom of the feet (which is called carrying); consequently, prevents the feet from touching the ground; until this, which forms a clog and is sticking to the feet, is worn off by a few steps on the sound ground, after leaving the ploughed land.

Another proof that the scent by which the fox is hunted by hounds does not come from the body, but from the touch, is that when hounds are running across an open country, downs, and such like, in very windy weather, it cannot be supposed even that the scent can remain stationary, but that it would be scattered by the wind; and that it arises from the touch, that is, the pad of the fox touching the ground. A person, to be more thoroughly convinced of this, has only to take hold of a fox's pad, or any other part when fresh killed, and the scent will be retained for many hours.

It is thought by some that the reason why

foxes are not oftener killed late in the day, after a hard and long run when it is nearly dark, that it is owing to their strength recovering as their natural time for exercise comes on; but the more probable cause for hounds not killing their fox oftener than they do at this time is that, as night comes on in the winter, the wind gets much colder, and the damp air, or rather the dew (which *falls* and does not rise, as some suppose, on any flat surface—for instance, the top of a gate will be covered with water by the dew, when the under-side is perfectly dry), depresses the scent, and prevents its expansion; consequently it becomes more difficult for hounds to feel it sufficiently to press a fox so much as they had done previously, although so much closer to him. And unless they do press him, it is almost impossible to say how much beaten he is; for it has happened often to the writer, who probably has enjoyed more of this midnight sort of scenery than most men, that when he has been determined to kill a fox, which from his running short and amongst the hounds in cover for a long time, it appeared that he was so beaten, that they would kill in a few minutes, the fox has, after dark, broke away, and taken an open country, when it has been necessary to stop the hounds, as it was impossible to see a fence. It should also be recollected that when hounds have run a fox till dark, they are not so fresh as in the morning, therefore the difference of the scent tells doubly on them; but if scent does return after a hard run, it is wonderful to see what courage and stoutness is left in a pack which appeared beaten. And it is one of the most rare events in hunting to see a *whole* pack quite beaten, although to casual observers they may appear so; but it happens occasionally, when they have this appearance after a very hard run and a long check, and have given it up, that the hunted fox has been moved, and it is then seen that those same hounds will run clean away from those very men who were probably remarking that the hounds were dead-beaten.

CHAPTER VIII

EARTH-STOPPING

HOSE countries which abound with fox-earths are very liable to have blank days, according to the usual method of management; for where there are earths, foxes at times will be in them when they are wanted elsewhere, even when the earth-stoppers do their duty. But the first question to put is, whether it is likely that a man can be depended on to get up long before daylight in the coldest and most dreary part of winter to stop a cold earth, and leave the warmer clay by his side? It is all very well for men to say, Yes! and that they know they do their duty properly, for they have sent down to ascertain it. Ascertain what? that the earths were stopped before it was light. What matters that? How long before light does a fox go to ground at this time, when it is not light much before eight o'clock, this being three hours later than at other parts of the season, and they are consequently more often stopped after the fox has gone in than before ;—and a very little ingenuity will extort this fact from an earth-stopper, that he has often found his stopping removed by a fox scratching out when he has gone to take it out himself next morning, which accounts for many blank days. This having been the writer's decided opinion from observation, ever since he has been a fox-hunter (and few men began more early in life), that immediately on his undertaking the management of a pack of fox-hounds, he commenced the following plan, to which he attributes the fact of his not having had more, upon an average, than three blank days in any four years that he kept hounds, although in the same countries from ten to twenty had been encountered previously in *one* year.

His plan was, in the beginning of October the head whipper-in went round to every earth-stopper, taking with him each day some matches, prepared as described on page 260. Or gas-tar may be rubbed against the sides of the earth within. Three days after this has been done, the same whipper-in should go round to every earth-stopper again, and see that he stops up every earth in the following manner: first, make a fagot of sticks the size of each hole, which should be thrust in, then drive a stake through it; after which, with a spade cover the whole over with earth. It may not be necessary to state it, but the reason why this last operation is not done at first is that, in consequence of the fox-earth being smoked by brimstone, a fox may, if in, not come out the first night; but by waiting three days he will by that time find his way out, and, consequently, the earth may be stopped without fear of stopping him in. After this is done, the earth-stoppers are to understand that the earths are to be kept stopped during the whole winter, until they have orders to open them in the spring for the vixens to lay up their cubs in—to be opened the last week in February. But if at any time previously in the season a fox goes to ground, half a crown will be deducted for every time any hole is found open,—which will be a sure remedy against going to ground. The earth-stoppers' pay will, of course, be under this new regulation reduced according to their deserts; but they will be as well satisfied as before, because they will have a regular salary, and very little to do for it, instead of being expected to be out all weathers when ordered, according to the old plan. The pay of an earth-stopper, notwithstanding this arrangement, can, at the master's option, be increased if he produces a litter of cubs in the woods which he looks over; and if he has a sovereign for every earth he has to stop and open in this way he will be satisfied. Some have two or three earths or more; but it must be left to the judgment of the master of the hounds. In the two countries hunted by the writer, the men were all satisfied although they did not get so much money; which was paid to them at an annual dinner in the centre of the country—generally fixing on some old earth-stopper to supply it, who keeps a public-house—at the rate of two shillings for dinner, and one shilling for drinking, each man.

The advantages gained by this plan are so numerous, that it has always appeared most strange that it has not been known to have ever been adopted by any other master of hounds. But it only requires to be made known, to become generally adopted; and as good sport was the great object of the writer in first doing it, he will have no difficulty in proving that it is a certain way to get better runs, because they are straighter, as the foxes do not run the rings they used to do—in trying every earth in the country where they are found—as they have already discovered that they are all blocked up, and therefore often go straight away. But, according to the old plan of merely stopping the earths in a certain quarter of the country the day it is hunted, when a straight, good run does happen, and the hounds deserve their fox, he goes to ground beyond the distance stopped for the day; although probably, had he not been able to get into the earth, he would have considerably increased the day's sport by going on some miles and being killed, which certainly is required to make a good run perfect—and all go home satisfied. In the next place, it is the best preventive against blank days; for, as before stated, many foxes nearly always lie underground, in bad weather particularly. Nothing is more common than when a fox is dug out to find a brace, or even more; and if these are found in earths so weak as to be broken up, how very much more likely is it that there are foxes in the main earths? Which accounts for every cover in a part of a country being drawn blank a few days only after snow, during which foxes were padded about in all directions, and no doubt were in the earths at the time the country was drawn blank.

The disadvantages of having earths are so much greater than the advantages, that if every earth in the country was done away with it would be a benefit to fox-hunting, even as respects the breeding of foxes, for the vixens would breed above ground in furze, or would find drains, which no one knows of, etc. But every fox-earth in the country is known to all poachers and fox-takers and keepers; consequently, every litter of foxes bred in them is known, and unless it is possible to have a constant watch over them, they may be taken in half an hour by various methods, none more fatal than terriers, which are taught to bring the cubs out alive in their mouths, or by digging pits at the mouth of the earth into which the cubs drop when they attempt to come out, which they will do shortly after they can see, in consequence of hunger, if the old vixen is kept away, who, poor thing! is watching close by, but dares not come to them, as one of these atrocious ruffians of fox-takers is near, ready to take the cubs when they fall into the pit. Added to which, the vixen often falls a victim to the keeper's gun at these main earths, for many have been known to place themselves on a tree over the earth, or near it, and so shoot the old vixen at the mouth of the earth; indeed, more keepers than one have been actually caught watching in a tree, with their gun, for that purpose.

But all this is avoided if the cubs are bred above ground as no man then knows where they are, till probably he has found them out by accident; and few men of this sort can prowl about in covers to find them without being seen. And if it does happen that they find them, probably they may be too young to take; and when they go again, intending to take them, the old vixen will have saved them the trouble, for if once a person visits cubs which are bred above ground, the vixen never fails to remove them. Also, when it is not known where they are, the old one has a better chance of escaping the traps, etc., which are so often found set. On one occasion the writer found no less than eight iron traps at one earth where a fox had gone in.

Independent of the above advantages of having no earths, or of having them stopped in this way for the season, there is not the same chance of having mangy foxes, for one mangy fox may infect half the earths in a country.

Another advantage of this plan is, that when the earths are opened at the end of February, although stopped till then, the vixen foxes will soon find out that they are open,—indeed they have been known to inhabit an earth which has been stopped within a week after it was opened, although it had been stopped the whole winter before; but the dog foxes not having the same motive for seeking the earths, do not find it out so soon, and consequently do not go to ground so readily as a vixen. Therefore if at this time, in March, there are earths open, it will probably be a dog fox which the hounds are running; and one of the greatest advantages of having earths at all, if not the only one, is that it enables hounds to hunt later in the season, as the vixens will generally go to ground. But this does not make up for the disadvantages; and it would be much better to lose a few days' hunting.

Having adopted this plan with the greatest success and satisfaction to all parties, although the intelligence at first to some gentlemen, when it was proposed by the writer, created much alarm, on his hunting a new country, with the dread that it would be the means of driving all the foxes out of the country, etc., which the fact of not having a single blank day for a year or two erased from their minds, it was no trifling addition to this satisfaction, and to the proof that earths are not absolutely necessary to have foxes in a country, for the writer lately to have had the opportunity of ascertaining that there are no earths in the whole Bedfordshire country, and yet foxes in abundance. It is very true, our forefathers did not stop the earths in this way; but in former times foxes were not bought and sold as they are now.

The only persons who really lose by this, are the old earth-stoppers; and they lose three things—first, their consequence by it in some measure; next, a few half-crowns for stopping; and thirdly, they lose a great deal of unpleasant work, such as getting up in the middle of the night, and going out in the dark, in all weathers; independent of which, they lose a great deal of abuse for not having done their duty.

CHAPTER IX

KEEPERS

Where there is a will there is a way.

HE sketch opposite is intended to represent a stoat being caught in a trap, baited in such a way that a fox could take the bait without being caught by the leg, as ninety-nine out of a hundred destroyed are caught—that is, when these traps are covered over, and the bait is on the ground under the trap. Independently of this plan preserving the fox, it is the most successful plan for all other vermin; and if all friends to fox-hunting were to insist on its being adopted, there would not be many blank days.

There is an old saying, "Give a dog a bad name

and hang him," which maxim is too often applied to gamekeepers; for there are some who are really friends to fox-hunting, and who have more pride in showing foxes with their pheasants, that is, in the same covers, than any others can have in showing pheasants without them. Innumerable instances

can be proved that foxes and pheasants can be had in abundance in the same covers, particularly where there are rabbits. The writer has seen five foxes cross a ride in a cover, and nearly as many hundred pheasants. Indeed, let any person go to Savernake Wood, belonging to the Marquis of Ailesbury,[1] or to Ashdown Park, which *swarms*

[1] This magnificent demesne extends to upwards of 4000 acres.—ED.

with pheasants, belonging to Lord Craven, and see these covers drawn by a pack of fox-hounds, and he will be convinced of the above assertion, for in the several years they were hunted by the writer they were never drawn blank; and it may be depended on, that the great objection which keepers have to foxes is that they destroy so great a number of rabbits, which are the keepers' perquisites, and consequently they are disposed to destroy foxes. It is a difficult thing to know how to act with them, but it is much the wisest plan to treat them civilly, even if they are doubtful, until proofs can be brought against them, that they do destroy foxes against their master's will; for there are many keepers, most highly respectable men, who have a right to expect to be treated civilly and respectfully. And indeed, under any circumstance, it is the height of folly to abuse them openly, as is too often done; it only exasperates, for they are generally men not easily frightened, at least if they are good for anything. The thing is, to prove that they do destroy first, and then go to work in every way, by applying to every friend and connection of the master's, and have it represented properly; when, if he, and even the lady of the manor, are inveterate against fox-hunting, she will, if it is properly represented, see how much more desirable it is to have all the mansions and residences in the country inhabited by families of a sociable disposition, in preference to their being vacant, which would be the case if there were no fox-hounds to induce men to reside in the country; and that those gentlemen who do preserve game monopolise so great a portion of the land, that only a few can enjoy shooting, but hundreds can enjoy hunting, whose whole sport and inducement to reside in the country is annihilated by this person's keeper killing foxes. Indeed, if there are ladies who do not approve of fox-hunting, the writer only requests that they will compare the private amusements of some men who do not hunt with those who do; for men must have some amusement, and it will be found, that the balance preponderates in favour of the fox-hunter; for instance, the following sketch. Shortly after breakfast, say nine o'clock, he leaves home, probably with this last request from his wife, " Do not forget to ask those several families to dine with us such a day"; which would not have been thought of, but owing to this chance of meeting them in the field, where he sees nearly all the best society in the neighbourhood, and returns after having had a good day's sport and plenty of exercise,—if through wind and storms, he enjoys his home so much the more. Dinner arrives, everything is capital, he is in the highest spirits, and he is happy with his wife and family. This is not always the case with some only who do not hunt. It is true they are also away all day, and return to dinner, but looking pale and wretched, having no appetite, and find fault with everything at table,— probably not forgetting the table they have been at during their absence. In short, men must be employed; and if they have no amusement in the country, it is natural to suppose that they will congregate, as abroad, in the metropolis, or a large town.

Although the scent was good, the writer thinks it right to whip off, for he has just discovered that many may suppose he had changed his fox, but he was only a little wide; and, as skirting is not approved of, he returns to the subject of the keeper, by relating a *fact* which will prove how very difficult it is to believe some of them. A gentleman who kept a pack of fox-hounds in the west of England (with whom the writer was on a visit just before the following circumstance had occurred, and afterwards) was desirous of preserving both game and foxes, as he always had done, and had just engaged a new keeper, who came from a suspicious quarter, and was therefore strictly ordered not to destroy a fox. As he kept a pack of fox-hounds, his orders were that the foxes should be more thought of than the pheasants; and the man promised most faithfully to obey this order, and take good care of the foxes—which he did, as the sequel will show. In a cover adjoining a park, two litters of foxes were bred up; and, during the autumn, the earths were occasionally visited by the master, with whom on one occasion was the writer. It was late in the autumn, and on a day after a wet night, when it was expected that the cubs would be padded near the earth, but nothing of the sort was perceptible. This created suspicion that all was not right, and the head-keeper was questioned closely. He said they were moved to another earth, and sure enough they were. The under-keeper was now made acquainted with this suspicion, and was instructed, unknown to the head-keeper, to search about the cover near where the cubs were bred. He did so, and found two places where the earth was fresh, and had evidently been lately moved. On turning it up, he found two beautiful healthy cubs buried, each with a leg broken, having been caught in a trap, which he at night put into a sack and brought to the gentleman, to whom he related where he had found them, etc. The headkeeper was sent for that night, and when he came into the room—called the justice-room, this gentleman being a magistrate—he commenced by expressing his suspicion that some unfair play had been going on with the foxes in the cover before described. The reply was, "That if there had been foul play, it was unknown to him; for he would not allow such a shameful thing on any account, and that he had taken every care possible of them." The gentleman then said, "I do not believe you; for I am sure you must have destroyed them." His reply was, "What! me, sir! I'll take my oath I have not killed them."—"Do you *mean* that?" said the gentleman. "Yes!" said the man. "Then take the book," holding out the usual Bible for that purpose to try him. He took the book in his hand, when the gentleman said, "Hold hard! my friend"; and rang the bell, when in walked the footman with the two young foxes, as before arranged. On seeing which, after a little confusion, and being asked whether he had ever seen them before, he said, "Well, then, I did do it, and I could not help it; for it would be unnatural in me not to kill what I was brought up to do." A severe reprimand and dismissal was, of course, the immediate result.

That a keeper should venture to kill a fox is bad enough, certainly; but that any other persons should think fit to do so is scarcely credible, when they know the loss it would be to the country if fox-hunting was destroyed. The writer was once with a very good man, and true fox-hunter, who addressed a respectable-looking man who was giving orders to some working-men on the road, in the following words: "Well, master, I am very glad to see you alive, which I did not expect after what I heard."—"Bless you, sir, I am very well; what could you have heard else?"—"Why, I heard that your son had shot a fox; and any man who would shoot a fox would shoot his own father!" In justice to this gentleman, it is fair to add, that a more liberal or kinder-hearted man does not live, notwithstanding this speech.

It is often dangerous to leave a fox which is run to ground, without making some arrangement so that no tricks are played; and the best plan is to give some man half a crown who lives near, and can be depended on, or whatever may be thought necessary, to go at night after dark to the earth, and find out whether any traps are set at the mouth of the earth. The writer has on more occasions than one had several traps brought to him, by the person employed to go there, which were found set at night, by keepers too who professed to be friendly. It is a good plan, if you run to ground and do not intend to dig, to move off with the hounds before any person on foot knows it.

Having finished this long chase with running to ground, the writer cries,—WHOOP!

CHAPTER X

STABLES AND KENNEL

THE following is a description of the ground-plan of the new stables and kennel for the Quorndon hounds, now building at Billesdon, Leicestershire, by Lord Suffield, according to the suggestion of the writer, whose intention was to combine comfort and convenience with economy :—

THE STABLE
contains standing for
41 horses.

24 stalls, 6 feet 2 inches by 18 feet deep, 12 feet high.

13 boxes, 9 feet by 14 feet and 4 feet behind, 12 feet high.

4 stalls for hacks, and coach-house, 9 feet by 14 feet and 4 feet behind, 12 feet high.

Saddle-room 16 feet by 18 feet (the fire heats the water in the cleaning-room).

Cleaning-room, 10 feet by 18 feet.

Forge, 10 feet by 18 feet.

Granary, 18 feet by 18 feet.

Store for hay, 18 feet by 18 feet.

Store for straw, 18 feet by 18 feet.

Also a covered ride 7 feet wide, inside the quadrangle; and in the centre a pit for manure and drains.

Over the entrance is one bed-room for men; a clock and weather-cock above, etc.

Remarks.—The mangers in the stalls are in two parts; one half for corn, the other for hay. Although the front of both is even, the part for corn does not go back to the wall, by about 8 inches, only 12 inches wide, and is 11 inches deep; but the part for hay does go back to the wall, and is 18 inches wide, and 18 deep; at the bottom of which is a narrow grating, to let through the seeds and dust. In private stables it is best to have a drawer below to catch the seeds, which would be valuable for pastures, instead of filling gardens with grass, etc., when carried there with the manure. The saving of hay is the greatest advantage of this plan, as a horse does not pull it down or tread on it as in *all* other racks, after which he never eats it; and the hay saved in one year will repay the expense of altering them to this plan. It is a more natural position for the horse, besides the prevention of hay and dust falling on his head and mane, etc.

The width of the stables is 18 feet, of which the boxes take about 14 feet, to allow a passage; but the entrance to each is made to open in the centre, so as to go back to the wall, to throw the whole 18 feet into the box, when desirable if a horse is lame or sick, or when thrown out of condition after the hunting season.

The covered ride is 7 feet wide; sufficient for two horses to be exercised under in wet or frosty weather.

The Kennel

No. 1. Young hounds' lodging-room, 16 feet by 20 feet; paved court, 18 feet by 20 feet; also a door opening into an enclosed grass-yard.

2. Hunting pack lodging-room, 16 feet by 20 feet; paved court, 18 feet by 26 feet.

3. Principal lodging-room, 16 feet by 20 feet; paved court, 30 feet by 34 feet.

4. Principal lodging-room, 16 feet by 20 feet; paved court, 30 feet by 34 feet.
5. Covered-court before feeding, 14 feet by 20 feet; at one end a cistern, to supply the kennel with water; at the other end a stair to the feeder's sleeping-room above.
6. Feeding-room 16 feet by 19 feet.
7. Straw-court after feeding, 22 feet by 24 feet.
8. Hospital for sick hounds, to be near so as to be fed often; three lodging-rooms, two, 6 feet by 6 feet, the other 12 feet by 12 feet, and court, 20 feet by 12 feet.
9. Boiling-house, 15 feet by 20 feet.
10. Cooler, 3 feet wide.
11. Coals, 6 feet by 10 feet.
12. Store-room for meal, 15 feet by 27 feet.
13. Straw-house, 15 feet by 21 feet.
14. Bitch-house, 6 by 15; court 9 feet by 15 feet.

Remarks.—All the doors, except those on the outside of the kennel, are in two parts, which open separately, which gives the opportunity of first looking at the hounds, and of seeing that no hound is injured on the feet by the door when opened against it. And the feeder can see better which hounds require to be fed first, on opening the top door.

The granary for oatmeal is placed for convenience, and to be dry, being at the back of the chimney to the boiling-house.

The straw-court, after feeding, is so placed, in order that the feeder may turn out every hound separately, if desirable, until the whole have been fed (this door should be in two, to enable him to look them over, and see if any want to be fed again), where they remain till he has time to walk them into the adjoining field. This is a most desirable acquisition to every kennel, as it keeps the field cleaner; and the droppings from the hounds make the straw valuable to farmers, which is taken from the lodging-rooms, and is otherwise useless. It is these considerations which make a farmer think it worth his while to supply straw for the manure.

It is also desirable that the hospital for sick hounds should be near the feeding-room, or they are not attended to as they ought, but are kept out of sight. Here the man has only to open the top part of the door and look in, and if a hound is in want, he has him in at once. This lodging-room is divided into three parts in case of any doubtful hound, which by putting aside, may prevent madness to the whole pack if attended to.

The door out of the young hounds' kennel into the grass-yard is intended to be open all day long, as it is most desirable that they should have room to exercise themselves when first brought home from their walks, before they are under command, which, by constantly taking them to be fed, they will soon come to. The time they are brought home is generally during the season when the men have not time to take them out, even if under command, which makes it so necessary for them to have an enclosed grass-plat to run over; and often prevents distemper going through the whole lot, as is often the case when they are confined close together.

There are pipes to convey water to every kennel, with a tap in each.

As before stated, economy in building these kennels and stables has been attended to, which the fact of the expense being less than half of a previous plan, designed by a first-rate architect, will prove; but it is fair to add that the first would have been a splendid building.

These kennels and stables are building at the expense of Lord Suffield, who is doing the thing on a liberal scale.

www.ingramcontent.com/pod-product-compliance
Lightning Source LLC
Chambersburg PA
CBHW032047220426
43664CB00008B/903